Acceptable Men
Life in the largest steel mill in the world

by Noel Ignatiev

CHARLES H. KERR
PUBLISHING COMPANY

ISBN: 978-0-88286-000-8 / e-book: 978-0-88286-002-2
Library of Congress cataloging in publication: 2021939149

Book design by J. Dakota Brown
Typeset in Roslindale by David Jonathan Ross
Cover photo by Paul Sequeira for the EPA (1973)
Author photo courtesy Rachel Edwards

Printed in United States on acid-free paper

Charles H. Kerr Publishing Company
8901 S. Exchange Ave.
Chicago, IL 60617
www.charleshkerr.com

It is not a question of what this or that proletarian, or even the proletariat as a whole, may imagine for the moment to be the aim. It is a question of what the proletariat actually is and what it will be compelled to do historically as a result of this being. The aim and the historical action of the proletariat are laid down in advance, irrevocably and obviously, in its own situation in life and in the whole organization of contemporary bourgeois society.

— Marx and Engels, *The Holy Family*

For gold is tried in the fire, and acceptable men in the furnace of adversity.

— The Apocrypha, Book 7, chapter 2, verse 5

Preface

Noel Ignatiev was a revolutionary his entire life. He drew his vision of a new society from *The Communist Manifesto*: "[Socialism is]... an association, in which the free development of each is the condition for the free development of all." Noel went on to write: "To understand that the emancipation of the working class is the task of the workers themselves, to take that statement literally... is the first demand of any individual or grouping of individuals that wishes to contribute to the emergence of the socialist society."

He believed that the path to revolution came not through some political party or trade union but through the day-to-day encounters of ordinary people with the exploitation and oppression that is part and parcel of the capitalist system. As Noel put it in the journal *Hard Crackers: Chronicles of Everyday Life* (which he founded):

"American society is a ticking time bomb.... In ordinary people in this country (and the world) there resides the capacity to escape from the mess we are in."

The role of revolutionaries like himself was to recognize and record day-to-day struggles of working people and to link these struggles that contained the seeds of a new society. Through his writings and his activism, Noel saw that the major impediment to these seeds actually becoming a new society is the institution of white supremacy and the social construction of race itself. The motto of the journal *Race Traitor*, which he co-founded, was "Treason to whiteness is loyalty to humanity." For Noel and others around him, revolutionary activity must be geared toward the elimination of the construct of race itself.

"The key to solving the social problem of our age is to abolish the white race," he wrote. "The white race consists of those who partake of the privileges of the white skin in society."

Noel, who had been raised in a communist family, dropped out of college in 1961 to pursue full-time activism. He worked at factories for 20 years, between 1963 and 1983, because he believed that this was where the day-to-day encounters of individuals with the capitalist system were concentrated at that time. He also joined Students for a Democratic Society (SDS) and served as one of its officers in 1969. During his time in SDS, he and another comrade penned an open letter denouncing the notion pushed by the Progressive Labor Party that workers should find the issues they could all agree on so as to "unite and fight." The letter that they called "White Blindspot" formulated the notion that "white skin privileges were the perks that were offered to white workers by the U.S. ruling class, in exchange for which these workers would forswear all meaningful solidarity with their non-white coworkers and bind themselves instead to a self-defeating alliance with the white ruling class." The task of the revolutionary, they argued, is to break this alliance.

As SDS disintegrated, he and eight other comrades founded the Sojourner Truth Organization (STO), whose focus at that time was revolutionary factory organizing where STO members would seek to contest white supremacy in both the factory and their unions. The objective was not to recruit factory workers to STO or to push an abstract political line, but rather to form "extra-union mass organizations at the workplace" around activities that would contest white supremacy and at the same time emphasize expressions of the seeds of a new society. Unions were seen as an impediment to this objective.

Noel worked at a number of factories. But in the early 1970s he went to work in the blast furnace division of U.S. Steel Gary Works, the largest steel mill in the nation. It was in the steel mills that the rawest expressions not only of white supremacy, but of the oppression and exploitation of the capitalist system were most clearly evident to all workers. Over his years at Gary Works he collected and participated in the stories of the day-to-day encounters of the working class with capitalism. This book is a collection of some of these stories. He does not do a political analysis of his experiences. Rather he takes you along with him and his coworkers so that you, the reader, can see the workings of white supremacy and capitalist exploitation, and also see the seeds of a new society in the workers' resistance to the capitalist system as manifested in the making of steel. Workers finding unique ways to be able to sleep on the job, for example, are questioning the imposition of sleep deprivation inherent in the work process at the mill. And they are saying, by extension, that in a new society, workers must not be subjected to sleep deprivation or the many other threats to worker safety Noel encountered in the mill. So as you read this account, ask yourself the significance of a group of workers meeting outside of the "guidance" of the union to determine what to do about a particular expression of white supremacy. What is the significance of a group of workers who are playing cards at work saying to a foreman who orders them to fix a particular machine, "can't you see we're busy?" What is the significance of a group of workers smuggling a broken boat motor into the mill that they want to use for fishing after their shift so they can put their heads together and fix it?

When Noel died in 2019, he left behind an unfinished manuscript containing the stories of his life at Gary Works. He was attempting to develop it into a novel but had discussed with friends and comrades whether it should be a novel or a memoir. He was concerned that all of his memories might not be exactly correct. He never kept a notebook of his day-to-day experiences and certainly didn't have a device to record his many conversations. Nevertheless, after reading what he had written, some of us decided it should be a memoir.

As for Noel's concerns about the truth of 45 year-old facts, memoirist Mary Karr stated:

> Of course, there's artifice to the relationship between
> any writer and her reader. Memoir done right is art,

a made thing. It's not just raw reportage flung splat
on the page.... From the second you choose one event
over the other, you're shaping the past's meaning.
    (Mary Karr, *The Art of Memoir*, 2015)

She goes on to say that writing a memoir involves using "novelistic devices like cobbling together dialogue you failed to record at the time."

Patricia Hampl describes memoir as a sort of family album that "doesn't provide a neat story line or even the facts but a collection of moments...."

Memoir, then, is only partly the work of telling a story,
it is also thinking about the meaning of the broken bits
of a story constructed from looking at the unsorted
snapshots, the shards of life.
    (Patricia Hampl & Elaine Tyler May, *Tell Me True*, 2008)

Noel found meaning in his experiences as a worker at U.S. Steel Gary Works. That meaning reflected his developing politics as a committed revolutionary who saw the possibilities of a new society in the everyday activities of his fellow workers. And he saw the very real threat to realizing the meaning of these activities at the hands of white supremacy. We are fortunate that he recorded these experiences so we can all learn from them. His story is most powerfully told in his own voice, sharing with us his reactions to the various "unsorted snapshots" as he experienced them at the time.

David Ranney

Acknowledgments

Charles H. Kerr Publishing Company is grateful to Noel Ignatiev for leaving us this wonderful account of his time working on the blast furnaces of "the largest steel mill in the world." A number of people greatly assisted the publication of Noel's memoir. So our thank you to:

All of Noel's comrades and fellow workers at U.S. Steel Gary Works

Kingsley Clarke

Rachel Edwards

The Editorial Board of Hard Crackers

John Henry Ignatiev

David Ranney

Amy Sanders

Tamara L. Smith

I

After the interviewer in the employment office nods approvingly at my application, he directs me to the plant hospital. There one man in a white coat checks my blood pressure, another checks my eyesight and hearing, and a third squeezes my testicles while I cough. He then peers into my rectum while I grasp my ankles. After all of this I watch a film about safety that shows several injuries so gruesome that two members of the audience are sick. Next I am issued a hard hat, safety glasses, and steel-toed shoes with metatarsal guards. I am led with two dozen other recruits onto a 1940s-era bus that drives through a gate under a massive arch with the name Elbert H. Gary etched on it. We are now on the grounds of U.S. Steel Gary Works in Gary, Indiana. It is the largest works of the largest steel company in the U.S. We come to a stop at a dirty, squat brick building with broken windows.

"Blast furnace maintenance office," calls the driver.

I jump to my feet, exit the bus and walk through the door of the office. A middle-aged white man in clean work clothes with "Marlowe" taped on his blue hard hat greets me.

"You're the new helper, here, eh? I'm the day foreman. Go with Poulos here," pointing to another middle-aged white man.

"Ever work in a blast furnace before?" Poulos asks as we leave the office. "Never mind. You'll catch on quick enough. Just be careful. There's a lot of ways you can get hurt around here."

We walk along a muddy, pitted road under bridges and overhead walkways until we come to a one-story building. Poulos pushes the door open and leads me into a room eighteen feet long and eight feet wide with gray walls, a row of gray-painted lockers on one side, a bench against one wall and a door opposite the one we had entered. He opens one of the lockers, takes out a coffee pot, fills it with water from a filthy sink, and sets it on a crude hotplate mounted on the wall between two lockers.

"Here's an extra cup," he says, pointing toward jars of instant coffee, sugar, and powdered creamer on one shelf of the locker.

While we sit drinking coffee, others come in, open their lockers, and make coffee. One man digs in his lunchbox, takes out a sandwich, and places it on the hotplate. About a dozen men stand or sit around drinking coffee and chatting. After about a half-hour, Poulos signals to me that it is time to go.

We put our cups back in the locker, and Poulos takes out a sturdy-looking cloth belt with a tool pouch hanging from it and fastens it around his waist.

"We're in the skip house today," says Poulos as we leave the shanty. "Keep your eyes open and stick by me."

Steel is an alloy of iron and carbon, sometimes with other elements. Iron ore and coke (made by heating coal in the absence of air) are combined and heated in the presence of limestone, which acts as a catalyst. The process takes place in a blast furnace. The result is molten iron, called pig iron (named after the molds into which it was traditionally poured, which resembled a litter of pigs). The molten iron is then carried to a second furnace where it is made into steel.

For the rest of the day I follow Poulos around, with no idea where we are or what we're doing but with better sense than to ask. Most of the day seems to be spent waiting for one thing or another, although in the afternoon, when Poulos says it's time to knock off, I realize I am very tired.

I report the next morning to the maintenance office, "home" to about fifty workers; about three dozen stand around each morning waiting to be sent out on different tasks. While the foreman goes from one to the other giving instructions, the rest stand around drinking coffee and talking. They range in age from just out of high school to ready for retirement. About a fourth of the men are black.

I am one of the first to arrive in the office, and take a seat on a bench to wait for the line-up. As the office fills up, one of the older workers comes over and tells me to get off the bench, that it is reserved for the four men in the department with the greatest number of years of service. It's known as the "hundred years bench." I get up immediately.

Again the foreman tells me to work with Poulos. I follow him to the shanty, where Poulos picks up his tool belt, and then on to the "skip house." As we enter I look at the huge blast furnace outside. It appears to be about 15 stories high and about forty feet in diameter. The skip house, Poulos explains, is where all the controls and motors for the furnace are located.

"We have four blast furnaces at Gary Works," Poulos tells me. "Today we work at this one. We need to check that the parts—brushes on the motors, relays on the control boards, and other devices—are functioning properly, cleaning or changing them as needed. The ability of the furnace to operate depends on us."

Much of our time is spent waiting for the furnace to fill so we can carry out our maintenance tasks. While we wait Poulos explains the basic operation of the furnace.

"Inside the furnace there are three stoves that heat air. This is what provides the blast that combines iron ore, coke, and limestone and turns it into melted iron."

I had heard about coke but was ignorant of exactly what that meant. "So what exactly is coke?" I ask.

"Coal is heated in a special furnace without air. All of that is done in another division of the mill. And they ship it over here. It is a very nasty place to work. As we go into the furnace area you will see what look like railroad cars. They are known as 'skips.' The skips are loaded underground with iron ore, coke, and limestone. They then travel by rail up to the top of the furnace and tip over, dumping their load into the top of the furnace. There are special doors at the top of the furnace called 'bells' that open and close. We will be called on to make sure they are operating properly when the furnace is down."

This is a lot to take in. And I am somewhat relieved when

Poulos decided to shift his topic from steel making to his complaints about everybody and everything.

"Let me tell you about these hotshots they got around here. Take Fletcher. He's your general foreman. I remember when he worked helper, back in the days before they had the PA. They used to blow a whistle: once for the millwrights, twice for motor inspectors. Sometimes I'd be working midnights with Fletcher for my helper and the whistle would blow and he'd be asleep on the bench. 'Let it blow,' he'd say. I'd have to carry him—he was real little then—I mean pick him up and shake him to get him awake. And now he's the general foreman, and if he catches you asleep he'll write you up. Let that be a lesson to you: never kick shit around, it's liable to be your boss some day. How old are you?"

"Twenty-five."

"Twenty-five. When I was twenty-five I thought I had a future. I had dreams, you know? I figured I'd be in the mill for a couple of years, and then I'd start some kind of business—maybe an ice cream parlor like the one I worked at for the Greek on Broadway. Now I got thirty-four years in this mill, and look at me, a dumb Greek. I could tell some of these geniuses in the office some things, but what do I care? If I was young like you, I'd get out of the mill. I'd start running and not look back. But you can't tell anything to a kid."

Suddenly he changes his tune.

"Everything considered, the mill has been good to me. When my wife had to have an operation, the insurance paid all the bills. I've been working steady since I started, not counting the strike in '59, and I've put my two girls through college."

"Some of these guys around here, these geniuses, they think they know everything, and if you fuck up a job they never let you forget it. Use your head, kid, it's natural to screw up once in a while, isn't it? I mean everybody makes a mistake sometimes. Right?

I nod, and Poulos continues.

"Well, some of these guys will ride you for years. I was a foreman once. I was foreman in the stockhouse. You know how long

I lasted? Three weeks. They got rid of me because I wouldn't kiss that Polack's ass that was general foreman. No offense if you're a Polack. Me, I'm a dumb Greek, so I figure it's all the same. Anyhow, they said I put too much stone in the furnace. But everybody's entitled to make a mistake. Even the law says every dog gets one free bite."

Poulos goes on most of the day griping about everything around him. It seemed he omitted few subjects. Most of the people and places he referred to went over my head, although a few names I caught and filed away. I decided to just keep quiet and nod or shake my head when that seemed call for. .

Silence must have been the proper response, because when we get back to the shanty for lunch, one of the other men asks Poulos how he likes his new helper and he replies, "This kid seems real smart."

After lunch, Marlowe, the day foreman, tells Poulos they would be putting his helper on shift work and that he should take him over to the supply house and get him fitted with a set of green clothes.

"That's the way you do it," complained Poulos. "As soon as I get a good helper you take him away and give him to somebody else. If you keep doing me like that I'm not gonna break in any more helpers. Let some of the geniuses you got up there break 'em in."

Marlowe smiles and ignores him. Poulos leads the way to the supply house, a room with shelves on the walls, located in the corner of a large building. A bald-headed fat man struts out of a back room, smiling and swinging his hips.

"What can I get for you, handsome man?"

"Give him two sets of greenies," says Poulos, "If you don't mind."

The fat man looks me over. "I would guess size large, thirty-two waist." He bats his eyes at me. "Is that right?"

I nod and say nothing.

The fat man goes to the shelves and returns with two heavy green cloth jackets and two pairs of trousers of the same material.

"These are for people who work on those nasty furnaces. Don't wash them in strong detergent or you'll destroy their heat resistance."

He then writes my clock number in large black letters on the back of the jackets.

"So they can identify your ashes," he grins.

II

The following day I report as instructed for the afternoon shift, going directly to the shanty without stopping at the maintenance office. From now on I will be part of a gang that rotates shifts or "turns." Instead of being given a specific task each morning, I am told to show up at my station, ready to take on whatever repairs become necessary.

I have been assigned to work with Jackson, the motor inspector. Jackson is a tall, heavily built black man with a deep voice and a hearty handshake. On meeting me he laughs and declares, "Finally I'm gonna have a white helper. You're gonna pay for the years of bad treatment I got from the whites when I was breaking in." The rest of the men in the shanty, black and white, chuckle. As usual I say nothing.

I am classified as a motor inspector helper. On first hearing my job title I thought it meant I would walk around with a clipboard taking down notes for the man who inspected the motors. Instead, I learned very quickly that the job involves making emergency on-the-spot repairs of anything electrical on the furnaces. A lot of it entailed changing light bulbs.

I soon learned that great overhead cranes bring coke, iron ore, and limestone from the docks and drop them into open railroad cars that ran along an elevated rail called the high-line. The cars in turn drop their contents through a grid into underground bins on both sides of a long tunnel. Underground, in the tunnel, known as the stockhouse, a rail car operator fills his car, called a larry car, from the bins, and the car then dumps its content through a door on the underside of the car into the skip, which runs on a rail up an incline to the top of the furnace.

Each blast furnace in the mill has its bins, its skips, its larry cars, and its three or four stoves. The stoves have valves that open and close in sequence, regulating the blast; these valves are powered by electricity and controlled by electric relays. Each furnace has a large drill on the casting floor for opening a tap-hole to let iron run out for a cast, and a powered ram, called a mud gun, to stop up the hole with clay when the cast is done. The mud guns are operated and controlled electrically. Overhead cranes on the furnace floor and other miscellaneous equipment are also powered and controlled by electricity.

To keep all this equipment operating properly was the job of the motor inspector. The six southernmost furnaces were called the South End. The six furnaces, high-line, stockhouse, transfer cars, larry cars, drills, mud-guns, cranes, and miscellaneous equipment on the South End were the responsibility of Jackson and me.

Szathmary is the foreman of the maintenance crew. He was five-and-a-half feet tall, of slight build, dressed in green like the others, and distinguishable only by the blue hardhat all foremen wore. He had started at the mill as a motor inspector, and felt more at home getting dirty among the men on the furnaces than in the office shuffling papers. He spent much of his time in the motor inspector shanty, where he drank coffee and ate his lunch.

The two other regular members of the crew are the millwrights, Vandermeer and Sourwine. They are expected to know something of the machinist's, rigger's, boilermaker's, and welder's trades. They change broken axles and brake beams on the transfer cars and cables on the cranes, and make sure that the doors, gates, and valves are operating as far as mechanics are concerned. They are the utility infielders of non-electrical work, as motor inspectors are of electrical work. The millwrights work hard, and were nicknamed jackasses.

Vandermeer is incredibly strong. On one occasion I tried to help him loosen a bolt. I could barely turn the ratchet wrench with both hands; Vandermeer pumped it with one hand as if drawing water from a well. One of the foremen had allotted him a chain-fail, a large piece of equipment with gears and pulleys used for lifting items too heavy to be lifted by hand. Vandermeer was proud of the loan.

"Remember the times I got the job done without having to go back to the shanty."

Jackson pointed out that now they would expect Vandermeer to lug the thing around with him whenever he went out on a job instead of being able to spend a half-hour going back to the shanty to get it when necessary.

The other millwright, Sourwine, is about the size of Szathmary, and wears the dirtiest set of green clothes I have ever seen in the mill. His face was streaked with grease, and before we shake hands he wipes the back of a greasy hand on his forehead.

My first assignment is to learn how to play hearts. As soon as all the men from the day crew clear out, and as soon as the silence of the PA system gives evidence that the supervisors from the office are gone for the day, Szathmary gives the signal and the men set up a card table from an old wooden box and a scrap of sheet metal that has been leaning against a wall.

"Do you know how to play this game?" Szathmary asks.

"I don't think so."

"Well, you just watch the first couple of hands. Dirty hearts is part of your job on my turn."

The game, as it was played on Szathmary's turn in the South End motor inspector shanty of the blast furnace division of the largest works of the largest steel corporation in the U.S., is a free-for-all game known as dirty hearts. Instead of partnerships as is the case in conventional hearts, each person plays for himself alone. If one player gets too far ahead of the rest, the other three will gang up to bring him down. Somewhere it may have been written that card games were supposed to be played silently; if so, the news never reached this game. The players freely discuss the cards they hold, and give generously of their opinions of the skills and individual moves of their opponents. None of this chatter reveals anything valuable, since it isn't possible to know who's telling the truth and who's lying. It is a game of cross and double-cross.

The men had agreed not to play for money, since they had seen or heard of sad things happening when people played cards for high stakes, including broken families and workmates attacking each other with knives. On occasion, usually right after payday, they agree that whoever fails to win a game in the course of the evening has to bring in a watermelon or ice cream for the whole crew to eat, but that was as far as the gambling went.

I watch the first few hands, and then in response to Szathmary's question offer the opinion that I am ready to try. As luck would have it, I win the first game!

"I guess we did right to bring him onto our turn," commented Szathmary. Everyone shakes their head and smiles.

Aside from the dirty hearts game there is little excitement on my first night, nor on the next. A couple of light bulbs to be changed, a fuse to be replaced on a larry car, that's about all. On our second night, while Jackson and I are returning from a minor call, I ask why they need two of us.

"I can't see why they keep two people on this job when it looks like there's not enough to keep one man busy."

"You'll find out," says Jackson.

The next afternoon I find out what he means. We had hardly got to the shanty when a call comes over the PA announcing a "skip stop" on number one furnace.

"That's us," Jackson says, as he puts on his tool belt and goes out the door, with me at his heels.

We head for the skip house where the control board is located. The control board is about eight feet high and ten feet long, and covered with what Jackson explains are relays. Each relay is labeled with letters and numbers. The relays seem to bang shut loudly and then fall open in some mystifying sequence I can't decipher. I remember that when Poulos first showed me the board a few days ago, my first impulse was to want to flee the room. This time I'm not afraid of it, but am no less bewildered.

"Despite the way they look," Jackson explains patiently, "all these relays open and close in a regular sequence. Each time one closes, it completes a circuit for the next, and this pattern controls the travel speed of the skip. If one of the relays failed to perform as intended, it means something's wrong. The problem is either in the relay or in the skip itself. In any case the skip is stopped, so we have to figure out which it is."

Jackson looks at the board, locates the relay that has failed to close, and pushes it closed. Immediately we can hear the skip begin to move and we wait until it makes its trip to the furnace top, tips over, and dumps its load.

We then go back to the shanty to wash up. Before we were able to take our belts off, Szathmary tells us that the stoveman on number three furnace had called while we were out, reporting he was unable to open the cold blast valve on number four stove. So out we go again. As we move toward the blast furnace, Jackson again explains our mission.

"Each oven in the blast furnace has a four valves that control how much air is released into the furnace. If they malfunction you can either get too much air or not enough. In any case, it will fuck up the final product. The problem is either with the valve itself or the switch that controls it. I'll show you how to check this."

Jackson leads the way onto the stove platform to check the position of the cold blast valve. We reached it by climbing a narrow stairway while holding onto a support rail. He climbs out on a railing and strains his neck around a pipe.

"The valve is right here. It ought to be open and it is. So there must be something wrong with the switch."

We then make our way to the relay room where he works the switch back and forth to loosen it up. When he does this we can hear the next valve start to move. The lights in the stove control room indicated that the stove is operating properly.

We take off our tool belts and hard hats and sit down on a bench. The stove man is an elderly black man, who moves with that peculiar flatfooted walk of those for whom the act of placing one foot in front of the other brings pain.

"How you doin', man?" Jackson asks.

"Feets hurt more than usual. Not sure why."

Suddenly the PA blasts out, "SKIP STOP ON NUMBER SIX! LET'S GO, BIG MOTOR INSPECTOR ON THE SOUTH END."

We put on our hardhats and tool belts and head for Number Six.

"That's Hooks, car man on six," Jackson says. "He always hollers like that. The other car men put him up to it. They tell him, 'Call that big motor inspector.' Sometimes on midnights you can get mighty tired of that voice."

We walk up the high-line toward number six furnace. It is late afternoon, the time of long shadows. Looking eastward we can see the channel where the ships carrying iron ore come in, and the docks where the ore is unloaded. Beyond that we can see the plant where coal is transformed into coke. To the north is Lake Michigan, which carries the ore freighters to the mill.

Jackson handles the skip-stop call without difficulty. Again we return to the shanty. Just as we finish a cup of coffee from the pot Szathmary had made, the next call comes. This time it's from the stockhouse.

The stockhouse makes me think of the model coal mine I saw during a visit to Chicago's Museum of Science and Industry. The stockhouse is underground, with a single set of rails running the length of the furnace line. On one side of the tracks is a walkway wide enough for two people. Slippery semi-finished iron pellets (known as taconite) are scattered on the walkway. I'm careful not to fall. The taconite pieces make walking treacherous. The ceiling is about ten feet high. Suspended from the ceiling is an energized rail carrying electric current to the cars that run on the tracks. Along the walls, above the top of the cars, is a series of bins for ore, limestone, and coke. The car man drives his car up and down the tracks, filling it from the bins that he opens by operating levers along the walls. When he has taken on a suitable load, measured by a scale on his control panel, he moves back and opens the doors in the underside of the car, emptying the load through an opening between the rails, into the skip waiting in the pit below. The dust in the air makes it impossible to see more than fifteen feet in either direction.

"Can't they do anything about all that dust? This has got to be hell on the car man down here for a whole shift."

"They've got water sprays that are supposed to keep the dust down," Jackson replies, "but half the time they don't work."

The car man on number two furnace called us because the compressor, which provides the air pressure that opens and closes the car doors, is not functioning. We climb up on the car, they see that the belt on the compressor is broken. Jackson sends me back to the shanty to get another belt. Meanwhile, he removes the compressor cover, which was bent out of shape and held in place with two rusty bolts. When I get back, we put the new belt on using a pipe wrench and a large screwdriver, and then replace the cover, using a hammer to drive the bolts in. By the time we finish we're sweating and dirty.

"This looks like one of those nights," says Jackson as we walk back to the shanty through the stockhouse.

The rest of the night is no better. There are a few more skip stops, another call to open the cold blast valve, some requests to replace light bulbs on the furnace floor, and a call to take one car off the track in the stockhouse and put another in its place. That job means we have to move five cars to get to the where the spare cars are located. We don't get to eat our lunches until it's nearly time to go home.

"Well, no card playing tonight!" Jackson says.

When the motor inspector and helper for the next turn arrive, we can barely drag our bodies off the bench and head into the wash-house to shower and change into our street clothes.

There are two shower rooms in the wash-house, each with a row of faucets along the walls. As I head into one, one of the men suggests that I shower in the other stall, since it has a mirror. Because I liked to shave after my shower, the suggestion makes sense, and I switch over. A few days later, when the wash-house was crowded with men from the day gang, I notice that all the black workers use the stall without the mirror. I begin to use the stall without the mirror, too, from then on. It's closer to my locker anyway. If any black workers resent my presence in "their" shower room, they never show it. In any case, while no black workers use the "white" shower, "whites" think nothing of joining me in the "black" shower when "their" shower gets too crowded.

III

Philip Greene is the youngest son in an old New England family. His father had been a lobbyist in Washington for the steel industry, and he himself had been brought up in metallurgy and furnace technology, in preparation for what was to be a brilliant career in steelmaking. Instead he is now in his mid-fifties and is stuck as a general foreman in the blast furnace division. Although he is in charge of production on six furnaces and has the power to discipline those who work under him, he works a rotating shift and gets dirty like a common laborer. He is bitter about the failure of the higher authorities to reward his breeding and education, attributing it to nepotism, or what he calls the "brother-in-law system." He regularly denounces the incompetence and favoritism in the administration, sounding much like Poulos, the motor inspector I worked with on my first day at the mill.

One night he had dropped into the motor inspector shanty for a cup of coffee and some conversation, as he often does in the course of his rounds. It wasn't long before he launched into his familiar diatribe about the "in-laws" who run things in the blast furnace division. This time, in addition to his usual complaints, he has some news for us.

"I hear they're bringing in a new hotshot to straighten things out in maintenance. The in-laws had a meeting last week and decided there was too much laxness in the maintenance crew. You can look for things to be different around here."

"When is all that supposed to happen?" asks Szathmary, who, as maintenance foreman, would be most immediately affected by any changes.

"That I don't know," replied Greene. "But from what was said at the meeting it shouldn't be far off."

He picks up the hand that had been dealt him and sits back in his chair. "Can't play long tonight. Busy, busy. Got a lot of work. That dumbass Moretti is blowing number one and two, and I can't leave him alone too long or he'll fill up all the blowpipes with iron."

The others at the table nod in mock sympathy. "They sure would have a hard time running this place without you," says Sourwine, the millwright.

"So what's the deal with Moretti?" I ask.

"Nothing wrong with Moretti," Sourwine replies. It's a shitty job. All of the furnacemen are in the same boat. There's constant problems with the furnaces. They have to know a hell of a lot and they're not trained for it. They face a lot of problems every day with no knowledge of what to do about them."

After Greene leaves, the men decide to take advantage of the lull to get some sleep. The millwrights return to their own shanty. I stretch out on the bench on my back. By this point I have learned to sleep on a hard bench with lights on and the PA system sounding off periodically. Jackson, whose length of service in the mill would have entitled him to the bench, suffers from back trouble and prefers to nod off sitting in a chair.

The hot summer days that have been so uncomfortable in the mill are giving way to the fall, the pleasantest time of year. In the weeks since I started work I have worked a complete swing around the clock and am now starting on my second set of midnights. As a result of all the shift changes, I have adopted the "steel-mill slouch"—a shuffle, shoulders bent and head down as if looking for lost coins, universal among non-supervisory employees within the gates of the mill.

At first I could not understand why it was necessary to change shifts every week, nor did anyone explain it to me. But after working each turn I figured it out myself. Blast furnace operation is continuous. Unlike an assembly line, the furnaces can't be shut down for the weekend. Three eight-hour slots every day times seven days means twenty-one turns each week. Each job, therefore, is rotated among four workers, with the twenty-first opening being filled by overtime or by a designated swing man who works a different spot each day. The solution is the system adopted by every steel mill—shift work—with shifts and days off rotated weekly. Some had suggested changing shifts monthly instead of weekly, or even the firehouse system—twenty-four hours on, forty-eight off—but given the eight-hour day and the five-day week, both of these would have required overtime premium pay.

Shift workers pick up their time cards from guards at the front gate and walk (or catch a shuttle bus) to their work stations, where they relieve the person before them. If the person they were to relieve was out on a call, his relief was expected to show up there. The foreman on each shift signs the time cards. Although the shifts officially began on the hour (8 a.m., 4 p.m., midnight), normally workers allow an extra half-hour for relief. A dinner or lunch break is not structured into the eight hours; workers bring food from home and eat when they can. Many keep canned goods in their lockers for emergencies or in case they worked overtime. One fellow was notorious for not keeping canned goods in his locker, mooching whenever he was called upon to work overtime; his workmates cured him by giving him a can of dog food, which they told him was corned beef. The relief system is a constant source of tension among the workers, since some are more reliably prompt than others. If a worker feels cheated he could exact retribution by showing up late for his turn, thus putting all turns "on the hour."

The system of picking up our time cards at the gates and having them signed by the foreman in the individual crew allows for a great deal of flexibility. At a nearby mill owned by another company, the management tried for several years to replace the system with one in which workers punched in at the entrance, as is the case in most industries. The workers responded with several strikes, which appeared a mystery to all those unfamiliar with mill custom. Why should people care where they hand in their cards? It turns out that many workers have private arrangements with their foremen which allow them to hand in their cards and then disappear for the rest of their shift. Having to hand in their time cards at the entrance to plant guards they did not know would have interfered with those arrangements.

Most workers who do shift work prefer it to straight days: "more free time to get things done" and "not so many big shots looking over your shoulder" were the most common explanations. One of the compensations of shift work is the chance to get a little sleep on midnights. Sleeping on the midnight turn is universal throughout the mill among maintenance workers. Occasionally someone in authority makes noises about the men sleeping on the job; the response is a chorus of snores. When I first came to the mill, I was puzzled by management's being willing to tolerate employees' sleeping on company time.

"No choice," explained Jackson. "They know that no one could work this schedule if they didn't get a chance to close their eyes on the job."

As I lay down on the bench I review the things I have seen since starting in the mill. Although I am far from knowing the job, I have seen nearly all of the blast furnace division: the highline, where men drive transport cars back and forth, dumping ingredients of the iron recipe through grates into the stockhouse bins below; the stockhouse, where other men drive cars through heavy dust, transferring the contents of the bins to the skip waiting in the pit below; the stove platform, where the controls are located for the great valves that regulate the blast of air into the blast furnace; the skip house with their immense motors capable of pulling a sixty-ton skip up a hundred-foot incline and operating the bells on the furnace top that prevent its contents from escaping into the sky; the complicated relay boards that control the motors; and the casthouse floor where men harvest the iron.

The work of many people in mines, coke ovens, and ore preparation plant culminates in the activities of about six men on the cast house floor.... It is at this point that lost time can never be made up.... It is the area where, in case of trouble, there is less dependence on mechanical aids, and progress depends on brute strength and stamina, where hammer, bar, and shovel are the principal tools in use. The wheelbarrow will never be entirely displaced in the cast house....

I like standing on the casthouse floor during a cast. An operator in a glass-enclosed booth moves levers that control an eight-foot-long drill, maneuvering it into the tap hole, and starts the screw turning. When the hole opens, sparks fly across the casthouse floor and the red-hot iron flows into troughs banked with sand. From time to time workers close a gate in one trough and open another, redirecting the iron into ladle cars that are open at the top. They then wait below to carry the iron to the next step in the process of making steel. When the iron has been tapped, and the cinder (slag: waste floating on the iron) has been run off, the clayman stops the hole with clay. Normally there were two or three casts per shift. Between casts, the furnace crew, working cooperatively, readies the troughs for the next cast and refills the mudgun. When this is done, they rest. The company considers it slack time but the rhythm of steel making is largely determined by the men on the cast-house floor.

Jackson tells me that years ago the U.S. Steel management tried to change this system by redefining and combining jobs in order to eliminate what they considered to be "empty time" between casts. Eliminating such "empty time" was to the management a time when their workers were not directly producing wealth for the stockholders. The workers responded with a three-month strike that left the existing job categories intact and allowed them a bit of freedom.

One of the first things I noticed about the blast furnace division was the amount of work the supervisors do—not merely "supervising" (standing with their hands in their pockets looking wise as in other industries)—but actual get-down, dirt-and-sweat, nothing-but-asses-and-elbows work. More than once I saw Szathmary come up to the skip house and get out the blueprints and voltage tester to trace the source of a problem, or work with pocket-knife and tape to make a quick repair. He won my respect both for his skill and his willingness to work hard. Not only the maintenance foremen worked. It was not unusual to see the stockhouse foreman down in the pit shoveling out spilled coal that was interfering with the skip's operation. Furnace foremen, called "blowers," routinely work, and so do general foremen.

One night I am sent to the casthouse floor with some light bulbs. The crew is changing one of the brass fittings that encircle the furnace and hold cooling water pipes. The fitting was burned up, and in order to put in a new one it was necessary to remove the broken fragments of the old one. The general foreman Greene stands in front of the fitting with a long, hollow tube on his shoulder, pouring flame into the opening. He puts the flame pipe down, picks up a high-pressure water hose, and with the help of one of his workers he turns the water on the fragments of the fitting. He then gets a heavy sledgehammer and pounds on the fitting until it comes off. Throughout the process the casthouse crew stand around leaning on their shovels, looking bored. I ask one of the maintenance crew why the foreman is working so hard.

"These niggers up here don't want to work," replies the man.

I reply: "I'm with them," and I sit down to observe.

IV

My reaction to the racist remark of the maintenance worker in the casthouse didn't come out of the blue. By the time I began working at Gary Works I considered myself a communist revolutionary. Going to work in the mill itself was for me a political act. From the time I was a youngster I knew I wanted to dedicate my life to revolution. What drove me to it I cannot say; my brother and sister grew up in the same home I did under similar conditions and chose to follow different routes. I sometimes think of myself as the product of an accidental coming together of molecules and vectors.

My grandparents on both sides came to America shortly after 1905, four among the millions who left Eastern Europe, cast out by the mechanization of agriculture. My father's parents, Jake and Celia, came from the Ukraine. My mother's father, Nathan, came from "Austria," which may have meant any place from Vienna to Galicia. My mother's mother, Reba, had been born in the U.S. of immigrant parents but had been taken back to Russia when she was an infant and later came over on her own as a young adult. Nathan and Reba were socialists and later communists, typical of those who in the cities of the east coast were the bone, nerve, and sinew of the radical movements from the Russian Revolution until after World War II. Nathan had left school to go to work at the age of twelve. It was hard times when he came to America, but he managed to save money to bring over his sister. Sometimes he slept in doorways; he told how it was often necessary to put his shoes under his head at night to keep them from being stolen. During the years I knew Nathan, he earned his living on a butter-and-egg route. He read the Yiddish press, mainly the *Freiheit* (the Communist Party newspaper), and the classics of world culture in Yiddish. The revolutionary movement was his school. His wife, Reba, died when I was five. I learned later she was a pillar of the Party apparatus.

Both of my parents were communists — my mother having been brought up in the Party, my father a bohemian radicalized by the Depression. They were largely self-educated, a testimony to the circles in which they moved. I grew up in a house full of books and classical music; dinner-table conversation was devoted to ideas.

Throughout my growing-up years, my father delivered the daily newspaper door-to-door — seven days a week for eighteen years without a day off, not even a Sunday. From the time I was eleven years old I used to get up at 4 a.m. three or four mornings a week to help him. We would work for a few hours, then have breakfast, which my father would cook. After breakfast I would catch a little sleep before going to school. The route was in a mostly-black neighborhood. My father used to say that there was not another white man in the city who could have handled it. Many of the customers would stop and tell me what a fine man my father was. I was proud to be doing a man's job.

On Sunday we would stop at the automat, which was a treat. Twenty years later I can still taste the sausages. One of the high points of breakfast was eating with the drivers who delivered the papers in bulk. I was fascinated by their conversation. One of them said to my father, "Good kid. Don't say much."

I attended a public college preparatory high school for boys, the same one my father had attended. Admission was by exam. One evening in the summer after I graduated, I was walking in the center of the city when I saw a man spread-eagled against a wall, being searched by a policeman. The man was black, the policeman white. When the policeman finished patting the man down, he bade him turn around, and when the man did so, slugged him in the gut.

I ran over and yelled at the cop: "You can't do that. You're not supposed to hit that man." The policeman grabbed me and threw me into a police car. I spent the night in a cell in the local station house. I was allowed to call home, and the next morning my dad showed up in court. When his case was called I tried to tell what I had seen, but before I could get out more than a few words, the judge interrupted, yelling that I had interfered with an officer. I was found guilty of something and fined twenty-five dollars. My dad paid the fine. As we were leaving the court an elderly black lady walked by and said, "God bless you."

I have felt blessed ever since.

I began college in the fall, but left after three years to take a job in a factory. I did so for two reasons: first, I wanted to be close to the working class, which I viewed as the revolutionary class of the age. Secondly, I wanted to help the class in its struggle for communism.

The first factory where I worked employed a couple of hundred people making the lamps that were suspended over the city's streets. My first job was as an assembler. After a few months I was upgraded to the position of drill press operator, at ten cents per hour more. There I learned my first lesson of factory life. My fellow workers taught me how to run the machine and also how to sabotage it when I needed a break. They taught me what was a reasonable amount of work to turn out so that I neither broke the rate nor let my fellow workers down.

My first goal was to fit in with my fellow workers. In order to do that I thought it wise not to let them know I had three years of college. That was easy, since no one expected a college near-graduate to be working there.

Now, ten years after leaving the university, I am working in the blast furnace division of U.S. Steel Gary Works, the largest works of the largest steel company in the U.S.

The Gary Works and the other mills in Southeast Chicago and Northwest Indiana were a natural target for radicals seeking to reach the workers. I belonged to one of the radical groups. It was one among several. Most of them were oriented toward gaining influence within the union. My own approach was distinctive. I had no interest in the union. Shortly after starting in the mill, I visited a well-known radical, who was president of the local union at a nearby mill. I asked him about the movement among steel workers.

"What movement?" he said. "There is no movement."

I knew that in the mill where the man worked it was common for the men to finish their work in half a shift and spend the rest of the shift in the tavern across the street. I asked him about that.

"So what? They've been doing that for years. It doesn't mean anything."

I had read about the history of the struggle for a shorter work day and I thought that the men spending their time in the tavern were doing something significant, but said nothing. I remember a rainy night when a foreman came into a shanty. I was sitting with a few other maintenance workers. Some were drinking coffee, some were playing cards, some were snoozing. The foreman asked two of them to see about a certain piece of equipment that was broken.

"Can't you see I'm busy?" said one, as he picked up the cards for the next deal.

"We'll get it when the rain stops," said another.

The foreman left, apparently satisfied that he had got the most he could from them at that moment.

In the midst of all this I had attended a national conference put on by another radical group. A couple of hundred people were present, nearly all ex-students; they all stood and introduced themselves by name and the number of the union local to which they belonged. When my turn came I stood and gave my name and the name of the mill I worked at, omitting any reference to the union.

The group I belonged to was a branch of an organization centered in Chicago forty miles away. The group called itself Sojourner Truth Organization (STO), named after a woman who had escaped from slavery in 1826 to become a famous abolitionist and women's rights activist. Our group in Gary consisted of a dozen people, mainly ex-students like me, who had committed ourselves to doing political work in the mill town. Some of us worked in the mill, a few in a local hospital. One worked for the welfare department, and one was a housewife. I fully expected that within two years we would either be "running the city or run out of town." We published a newsletter, *The Calumet Insurgent Worker*, reporting on things that were happening in the area and around the world, and distributed it widely in the mill. Jackson said it was the best of the little radical papers that occasionally found their way inside. It differed from the others in two respects: first, rather than preaching at workers, it was a place where their voices could be heard. For example, the second issue ran a letter from a mason who worked at one of the mills in which he lamented the lack of support from other workers when the masons went on strike for 117 days. The next issue carried a response from another worker who asked why the masons had their own union. "It is true," wrote the correspondent, "that the steelworkers' union isn't worth a damn, but still it isn't right for one small craft to cut themselves off." He wondered how many blacks and Puerto Ricans are in the masons' union; he never saw any on the picket line. The second difference with the usual radical papers was that *The Calumet Insurgent Worker* sided unequivocally with the black workers, even at the risk of offending whites.

I was especially proud of an article I didn't write but merely "found." U.S. Steel Gary Works published a newsletter aimed at the employees, written in a cheery style. One of the articles in it told the tale of a woman whose husband and children had worked at the mill over decades, sometimes as many as six at once. She recounted her life of packing lunches and dinners and washing work clothes, and concluded, "I, too, feel as if I had worked for U.S. Steel." I was certain the editor of the company newsletter was aware of the irony. *The Calumet Insurgent Worker* reprinted the article without comment.

When workers at the nearby auto plant went on a wildcat strike, I drew up a leaflet calling upon workers at the mill to show up at their picket to support them. STO distributed it at the mill gates. So far as I could tell, there was no response.

When a couple of autoworkers at a Chrysler factory in Detroit took over the power station and shut the place down, I went to Detroit to get in touch with them and invite them to Gary to speak. Our STO branch set up a meeting for them at a local church and arranged for flyers to be passed out at the mill announcing the meeting. Only the organizers attended.

We held a meeting at the same church for Mississippi pulp workers, black and white, who had organized an independent union and gone on strike and were on tour to build support. That one was better attended — maybe a half-dozen people apart from the organizers. *The Calumet Insurgent Worker* printed a letter from a black steelworker who attended the meeting:

> Their story was interesting, but several things about
> their presentation bothered me. Their leader mentioned
> several times that the black woodcutters had been slow
> to join in the strike and that they had furnished some of
> the worst scabs. I think if he was going to tell these things
> then he should tell why. It wouldn't hurt anyone's feel-
> ings to hear the truth. I blame myself for not asking him
> during the question period. I guess the reason I didn't
> was because I already knew the answer: the black people
> in Mississippi have been betrayed so many times by
> whites that they are not going to rush into an organiza-
> tion that was started by whites even if it looks like it is
> to their advantage. I also didn't like the way the white lead-
> er of the group jumped in and answered all the questions
> from the audience. I could understand the two women
> being shy, but I talked to the black man afterwards and
> he seemed able to speak for himself. The group seems
> to have learned the need for working together, and that
> is good. But there is still a long way to go.

Around that time, owner-operator long-distance truckers went on a shutdown protesting high fuel prices. All over the country, they pulled their rigs into truck stops, turning them into centers of organization. Because in many cases they chose to pull in close to where they lived, their wives and girlfriends began showing up. The Gary Works was close to the intersection of two major inter-state highways, and the truck stop at the intersection became one of the centers. STO members moved temporarily to the truck stop to work directly with the strikers. One of our first actions was to help the truckers design a poster, showing a photo of an actual striker's truck at the truck stop, with a sign in the driver's window that read "Shut down until..." We printed the poster on STO's press, and distributed it widely at the stop and in the Chicago area.

In addition to printing the poster and talking with the wives and girlfriends of the truckers, STO members helped the truckers make contact with women living in the area whose husbands, brothers, or sons had shut down in other parts of the country. We hoped to persuade the strikers to broaden their demands to address not merely fuel but food prices. We also sought to build links between the strikers, largely white men, and people of Gary, whose population was largely black, by pointing out that we all shared an interest in keeping prices down.

I recall a meeting at a member's home, at which a black trucker reported that one of the whites, seeking to protect his rig and not recognizing him as a fellow driver, had leveled a shotgun at him when he was walking through the truck stop. I thought the presence of a black trucker at that meeting was a major achievement.

For a short time the work stoppage had a national impact, forcing the government to call out the National Guard in some areas. STO was perhaps the only radical group in the country to take the stoppage seriously. In part our support was due to the fact that it reflected our vision of mass organization independent of the unions. As owner-operators, the truckers were formally self-employed independent contractors who could not have formed a traditional union even had they desired to do so. But also we were attracted to this struggle because of its reliance on direct action rather than negotiation.

In the end, the strike petered out, as the truck stops emptied and the truckers returned to the road. I thought the experience proved that a small group could have a big impact, and speculated that if a group like STO had existed nationwide, the outcome could have been different.

V

I am suddenly awakened from my nap on the hard bench by the PA.

"SOUTH END MOTOR INSPECTOR, COME TO NUMBER THREE CASTHOUSE! CAN'T GET THE MUDGUN INTO THE HOLE! SOUTH END MOTOR INSPECTOR, CAN'T GET THE GUN INTO THE HOLE ON THREE!"

Jackson and I jump up, grab our tools and head toward Number Three Casthouse. No call could be more urgent. The mudgun is used to plug a taphole that seals a furnace after a cast, keeping molten steel inside the furnace. If the flow can't be stopped at the proper moment it can run down the troughs and over the top of the ladle cars, pouring onto the tracks below. Such accidents have led to serious injuries and deaths. They also make a giant mess and put the furnace out of commission.

Arriving on the casthouse floor, we can see that the gun used to plug the hole is in front of the taphole where it is supposed to be. But the barrel of the gun is not in position to drive the clay into the hole. Red-hot metal is flowing out of the taphole.

"Go to the control room, count to sixty, and then operate the ram, forward and backward," Jackson shouts. "Do it a couple of times each way."

I raise my arm to shield my face from the heat and jump across the trough flowing with hot metal. Inside the control room I locate the proper lever, wait, then shove it into "forward" position, peering through the dirty glass for any sign of movement in the gun barrel. At last I see the ram slide forward. At the same moment I see Jackson in the big door of the casthouse, hardly visible through the clouds of dark smoke. I signal to him by waving my arms back and forth across my chest.

"I think that's it," I tell the clayman standing next to me at the controls. The clayman takes over and I go out.

"One of the tips on the relay was burnt and wasn't making contact," says Jackson. "I held it in so they could work the ram. When they finish plugging the hole we'll fix it."

We stand at the edge of the casthouse floor, watching. Several of the crew are wearing floor-length asbestos cloaks and hoods with glass masks. They move slowly. The river of iron breaks into rivulets and disappears in a hole in the floor. The air is heavy with smoke. I am wondering if Dante had worked in a blast furnace. I know that Dickens once described a steel mill as "hell with the lid off."

It takes about ten minutes to plug the hole. When they are done, Jackson takes me out to the skiphouse and shows me the faulty relay. He pulls the power switch on the board.

"See, this tip here fell off and wouldn't let the acceleration come in. We'll have to replace it."

He takes a shiny tip out of a cabinet filled with a jumble of spare parts. Deftly, he removes the defective tip and replaces it with the new one.

"That should do it. Let's see if it works." He puts the power switch back on and then leads the way back to the casthouse. From the edge of the floor he signals to the clayman in the control room to pull the ram back. The clayman pulls the lever and the ram slowly moves back.

We walk back to the shanty along the highline. Dawn is just breaking over the coke plant in the east.

"Don't you get a good feeling," I ask, "walking the highline on a nice morning when you've done some real work that had to be done to keep the place going?"

"I think everybody who works here feels that," says Jackson.

Back in the shanty we pour ourselves the last cups of coffee and I put the pot in the sink; it was my turn to wash it. While we are drinking our coffee, I ask something that has been on my mind for a while.

"Do you remember the first day when I came to work with you?

You said how glad you were to have a white helper so you could take out on him what had been done to you when you first started out. What did you mean?"

"Aw, I was just fooling," says Jackson. "I wouldn't do that to anybody."

"I can see that, but I'd still like to know what you were talking about — that is, if you don't mind telling it."

Jackson is silent for a few minutes. "Man," he says, "once I get started I don't know if I can stop. I started in the mill as a laborer on the docks. The Company posted a job for a bridge operator — you know, those big cranes that bring the ore across the channel to the highline. Well, I bid on the job and I had enough seniority to get it. So they sent me up on the bridge and the operators up there — they were all white — were supposed to break me in. You know they wouldn't do it? They wouldn't let me at the controls. Kept telling me I wasn't ready yet. They wouldn't even let me see them while they operated the bridge. They would block the controls with their body so I couldn't see what they were doing."

"These were guys I had worked with, you know? We had eaten together, and kidded around the way people do, and even shared food. Finally, after a week of this, one guy comes to me and says, 'I know what's going on. You work with me on Monday and I'll break you in.'

"At last, I thought, I had found one decent one in the bunch. On Friday afternoon, though, he came to me and said 'I'm sorry, man. I can't go through with it. It's bad enough that these guys out here have quit talking to me, but my own wife called me a nigger-lover. I'm sorry, I just can't go through with it.'

"I never did get that job. And I had five babies at home.

"Years later I got to be motor inspector. When I told them I wanted to bid on the motor inspector job, they tried to get me to switch to millwright, or welder, or anything. At that time the motor inspectors were all white, and the management wasn't ready to open the job up. Well, I kept insisting, and I had more time than anybody else who bid on the job, so they let me have it. A lot of these guys who are so friendly now wouldn't talk to me back then.

"My first helper was white. One day we got a skip call and I went up to the skip house, and I couldn't get that skip started for anything. I mean, I tried everything I knew and I still couldn't get it to go. Finally, I went behind the back of the board and I saw that a wire had been pulled off and that was why the skip wouldn't go. I put the wire back where it was supposed to be and the skip took off.

"As I was leaving, one of the guys from the furnace told me he saw my helper leaving the skip house just before the skip stopped. He knew I had a white helper."

"What did you do?"

"What did I do?! I went back to the shanty and I told him that if he ever pulled any shit like that again I would cut his mother-fucking throat."

"What did he say to that?"

"Aw, he denied knowing what I was talking about. But I never had trouble from him again. I still see him once in a while. He's a motor inspector on the docks, and he greets me like we're old friends.

"Let me tell you, you see a lot of us now in the motor inspector gang, but it didn't use to be like that. When I first started here, hardly anybody would even speak in the shanty. You know who broke me in? The car men in the stockhouse, and the stove men on the furnaces, that's who. I didn't know a thing about those stoves, and every time I'd ask somebody in maintenance they'd be too busy to explain. When I got a stove call I'd have to go up there and figure it out with the stove man. They remembered how hard it was for them, and they helped me.

"One thing I'll say about Red—a lot of the guys complain that he's a hardass. When he saw how hard I was struggling he took me on a tour of the stoves and explained the valves and showed me where they are on the print. He may be a hardass, but he was the only foreman that showed me around."

"Every one of us out here has stories like that. You know Moore—he's motor inspector on the North End. When he first bid on the job they gave him a test that an electrical engineer couldn't have passed. They admitted it, but they said they were within their rights because it was stuff that might be part of his job. He flunked the test, naturally, and it was another five years before he made motor inspector. And in the meantime Poulos and some of these white motor inspectors don't even know how to read prints."

Jackson grew up in New Madrid County, in the Boot Heel of Missouri (so-called because of its shape). Until the early 20th century, the district was largely covered by wetlands and swamps, but otherwise was a wheat-growing area of family farms. Lumbering was important in the 1890s until the most valuable trees were taken. After the boll weevil ruined the cotton crop in Arkansas, planters moved into the Boot Heel, bought up the new lands or leased them from insurance companies that had invested in the area, and recruited thousands of black sharecroppers as workers. In 1935 three-fourths of all farms were operated by tenants, most of them black.

Jackson's father was born in Mississippi in 1909. As a boy he walked three miles to school every day; he left in the fourth grade. At 14 he came to southeast Missouri. He first worked in the cotton field plowing behind a team. He got $1.25 a day, from March until April 30. How many hours a day did he work? "All."

In June the cotton chopping began. Again he got $1.25 a day. This lasted until the middle of July. There was no more work until the last week in September, when the picking started. This was piecework. Every 100 pounds, 75 cents. Some strong fellows picked 200 or even 250 pounds. The average man picked 150 pounds. The women would pick about 100 pounds. This stopped in December and there was no more work until the next March. He lived in an old shack. When it rained he couldn't sleep, for the water came in, summer and winter. This was his life to 1937. In 1935 he heard of the NAACP through the local preacher. He joined. There were about 100 members in his local. He and his wife made a crop in 1938. They farmed 11 acres. Starting January 1 they got $12 a month for five months. The landlord furnished mule and plow and fed the livestock. In September they started to pick. He made nine bales at 500 pounds a bale. The total amount was $405. His share was therefore $202.50 minus an advance of $60 and other minor advances.

In December when he was paid off he got $4.55. His brother was making a crop for the same landlord. In June his brother got a job on the WPA at $8 a week and left the crop. Jackson's father took over his brother's crop and made nine bales of cotton. The $4.55 he received was for both crops.

The practice of stealing by the landlords varied from state to state and district to district. But there was scarcely a black man in the area who did not know that he must work a few months of the year, all hours of the day, for $1.25 a day (when it did not rain) or do share-cropping and be at the complete mercy of the landlord.

In 1934 the Roosevelt Administration passed the Agricultural Adjustment Act, aimed at cutting down the acreage of cotton by one-third. The government set a price and paid the farmer the difference between that and what he got on the open market. The surplus, millions of bales, was stacked in government warehouses. One-third of the crop was to be plowed under, and soil conservation payments were made to the landlord, providing that the money advanced by the government should be shared by the farmer.

The law provided that the landlord could not make any change in his condition of ownership, etc. But the landlord evaded this provision by making a bogus sale to his brother or a friend and fixed things up to suit himself. The county committees responsible for working out the details were landowners themselves or friends of landowners.

By 1938 the landlords calculated that if they had no tenant farmers and no sharecroppers they would not have to divide the government's subsidy with anybody. In January 1939 the landlords in southeast Missouri told the sharecroppers to vacate their shacks. They had nowhere to go. Some of them scattered and sought refuge with a brother here or a cousin there or a friend somewhere else. Where a two-room shack had housed four persons, it now housed six. Families broke up.

One thousand five hundred families, black for the most part, with a few whites, camped on the St. Louis highway. They took their scanty possessions with them and announced their intention of staying there until the government took some steps on their behalf. Police, armed to the teeth, came to intimidate them and make them leave the highway. The sharecroppers, who had their guns with them, resolutely refused. The Health Department and the Humane Society came out and investigated. The sit-down strike was called a menace to public health. The chief of police and other officials came to get the strikers to move on. The result was nil. There they were and there they were going to stay.

Of twenty thousand day laborers in that part of the state, about five thousand took part in the demonstration. It was the first attempt at mass action. After three generations, the black people in the Boot Heel had had enough. It was bitterly cold, and they lived in tents or in the open. Babies were born on the highway. About two weeks later they had to give in. They were shepherded away into livery stables, schools, broken down public buildings, and holes and hovels of all kinds. A very small percentage of the landlords took croppers back, and some were lured back to the cottages on the promise that they would not be charged any rent. On July 1, however, eviction notices were served on them, and some went to jail. The majority lived how they could, but most of them went back to work as day laborers.

A group of ministers in St. Louis formed a support committee and about a hundred miles away found a piece of land, infertile and rocky, at the top of a hill in the county of New Madrid. Three hundred and five families made the trek to it, and they began life over on July 3, 1939. About a thousand people lived on bread and gravy for two months. The local relief committee gave them as little as possible, hoping to throw them out. The sheriff threatened them. However, they stayed at the camp, Poplar Bluff, and they built a village. Of the three hundred and five families who went, five were white. Jackson's father was one of the leaders. Jackson's family was among those at Poplar Bluff. Jackson was eight years old.

After the demonstration his father went back to work. This time he and his family lived with two other families in three rooms. The pay was $1.00 a day. The landlord was using tractors, not horses. He needed labor only for chopping cotton and picking. Where one man used to do 10 acres a day, the tractor did 33. The landlords had succeeded in reducing the number of laborers.

With the approach of World War II the country began to emerge from the Depression. Rearmament brought jobs. Many black families left Southeast Missouri. Jackson himself was too young to leave. Ten years later, the outbreak of the Korean War further increased the demand for labor in the steel industry. In 1951, at the age of twenty, Jackson came North.

He was one of four brothers and two sisters. One of his brothers went to Detroit, where he got work in the foundry at Ford. Jackson went to Chicago and Gary. Another brother took up the burglar's trade and wound up in prison, and one stayed home, eking out a living doing odd jobs. One of his sisters moved to St. Louis, where she became a school teacher, and one stayed home, doing domestic work for white families.

Jackson married a woman, also from the South, whom he met at a social sponsored by the Church of God, to which they both belonged and which she attended more regularly than he. At first she worked as a nurse's aid in the city hospital, but as children came — five in all — she left the job to stay home. Jackson worked pretty steadily throughout the 1950s and 1960s, including every hour of overtime he could, except for a brief layoff in 1958 and the three-month strike in 1959. His wife was a good cook and housekeeper; the family lived frugally and were able to save money and buy a home on the west side, not far from that other Jackson family which would become world-famous and whose patriarch also worked in one of the steel mills in the region. By the time I started as Jackson's helper, three of Jackson's children were enrolled at the local community college, with two more still in high school.

One of the other motor inspectors, Tom Allen, had a contract delivering TV sets to the local hospital. To supplement his income, Jackson helped him, but quit after a few months. He explained,

"I found out that Allen's son was skimming. I didn't want to tell on him to his father, but I figured I better get out before I got caught between them."

VI

The phone rings, and Jackson answers with the customary "South End."

"That was the maintenance office," he says after he hangs up. "They want us to stop in after we're showered up. They're goin' to have a meeting."

When we get to the office the whole maintenance gang is there — motor inspectors, wireman electricians, millwrights, boilermakers, riggers, welders, and even the machinists from the metal shop and carpenters from the wood shop — a hundred-odd men. Most are in work clothes. Jackson and I, having just come off the midnight turn, are in street clothes. There is a hum of voices, interrupted by an occasional laugh.

Fletcher, the general maintenance foreman, stands in front. At his side is a man I have never seen before, wearing a clean green furnace jacket over a white shirt and necktie.

"Can I have your attention, please," Fletcher shouts. When the noise subsides, he continues. "We called you together for several reasons. The first is to talk about safety."

"It will be getting chilly soon and, as many of you know, they will be turning on the steam in the stockhouse. This can lead to steam leaks on the road you take to the shanties. The leaks make visibility difficult. Since the road is also used by the trucks that carry flue dust, as well as other vehicles, it creates a potential hazard. In the past, people walking on the path have narrowly escaped being run over. Therefore we are instituting a new essjaypee: people are requested not to use the road to reach the shanties. It is permitted to cross the road when going from the shanties to the furnaces, but for longer trips use the stockhouse or the highline walk. Questions?"

"What's an essjaypee?" I whisper to Jackson.

"It stands for safe job procedure."

A hand shoots up. "Yes, Mays?"

"What about the pellets on the stockhouse floor? Suppose we slip on the pellets and fall?" Mays is the union representative for the department. Raising objections at safety meetings is his way of demonstrating that he is defending his constituents' interests.

"All persons walking through the stockhouse," replies Fletcher as if quoting a regulation from memory (which, in fact, he was), "are required to exercise caution due to the presence of pellets and other hazardous materials. When the steam clears, you can go back to using the surface road."

"That won't be 'til the spring," grumbles Mays.

"Another safety measure concerns the new furnace. As you know, construction has begun on a new blast furnace, number thirteen, at the far north end. It will be the largest and most modern in the western hemisphere. During construction there will be workmen from the contractors as well as earth-moving equipment and other vehicles at the scene. Those of you whose job does not require you to be in the area are requested to stay away. Guards will be posted to keep out all unauthorized personnel. I know that you're all curious to see how the work is going, and everybody likes to watch. I know I do myself (said with a smile intended to communicate fellow-feeling), but you will not be permitted in the construction area. However, tours will be organized under safe and supervised conditions."

"Now I'd like to introduce the gentleman standing on my right, whom some of you may have seen and wondered about. His name is John Hemple, and he has come here from Pittsburgh." His voice is lowered appropriately.

"Thank you, John. American steel manufacture," he begins in a corporate tone, "is involved in a war. The war is being fought in the markets of the world. It is not yet determined whether our country will win this war. Many of you have images of Japanese steel industry as backward and inefficient. That image is inaccurate; they possess the same modern technology we do. They are rapidly approaching our levels of productivity. Since their wages are lower than ours, they have been able to undersell us and win away markets we thought were securely ours—even right in this country.

"Our goal in the war is to improve productivity—to manufacture high-quality steel at lower cost than our competitors and thus maintain America's preeminent position in the world market, and the prosperity—full employment and high wages—we need to maintain our way of life.

"In the battle for high productivity, U.S. Steel Gary Works occupies a crucial position. It is the company's largest works, and, indeed the largest steel plant in America. Statistics gathered and examined in recent months indicate that this works is not operating as efficiently as it should. We have a right to expect better. It is our belief that the blast furnace division, and in particular the maintenance department of that division, is key to the turnaround, since the blast furnace is the foundation of the steelmaking process.

"The Company is doing its part. Construction has begun on a new furnace which, as John told you, will be the largest and most modern in the Western Hemisphere. Together with the new continuous casting mill and the new basic oxygen furnace, both of which have been completed within the last three years, it will give this works the greatest steel-producing capacity of any in the free world.

"It is not enough to sit back and allow the company to carry the burden. Each and every one of you has a role, as important as the one played by the new equipment. It is your part to ensure that maximum use is made of the equipment the board of directors has chosen to erect here.

"I am convinced we have a fine crew, able to meet the challenge we face. Over the next few weeks I will be going around observing various aspects of the work, seeking ways to improve our methods. I am sure all of you will extend to me your fullest cooperation, so that together we can improve our performance."

As he drones on an image flashes across my mind of a routine I saw on TV in which an old comic wearing baggy trousers and a crushed fedora is explaining in what purported to be a New York accent, "I gotta job to do, and you gotta job to do, and if you do your job, and I do my job, then togedda we'll get the job done, togedda."

As I look around the shop, most of the men are staring poker-faced at the two Johns in front. Poulos is looking at a spot on the wall, bored. One man is digging in his ear with his little finger. Another is massaging his crotch with a faraway look in his eyes. Two men in back, out of the speaker's view, are studying a magazine with colored pictures of naked women. Vandermeer is listening closely, nodding his head in agreement whenever the speaker emphasizes a point.

"Remember," continues our man from Pittsburgh, "in the final analysis the outcome will be up to you — to every individual in this room. Only you can maintain the strength of the American steel industry."

"I guess that's all, John, except that I look forward to seeing and talking with the men out in the field, and taking part in the general efforts to raise the standing of the team."

"Thank you, John," says Fletcher. "I'm sure all of the men here will be glad to cooperate, as they understand how crucial this battle is. OK, men," he says turning back to the audience, "that's it for the meeting. My thanks to you for attending, especially to those coming off the midnight shift. I'm sure you're all eager to get home to breakfast and bed. You'll find an extra hour's wage on your next check. Marlowe," he says to the day foreman standing in the doorway, "you can go ahead and line up the day gang."

VII

That night, as we are setting up the table for dirty hearts, we discuss the meeting.

"It looks like Greene had the right dope about this new guy from Pittsburgh," Sourwine remarks. His green suit is black from coal dust, and his face streaked with grease as usual. He is sitting at the card table with Jackson, Szathmary, and me. Vandermeer sits on the other end of the bench, a cup of coffee in hand.

"I wonder what kind of changes they've got in mind," says Jackson.

"I told them in the office," Szathmary adds, "that so far as I'm concerned we have a pretty job-conscious crew on this turn. We get the job done."

Vandermeer, on the other hand, argues that the speaker made sense. "Look at the radio and TV industry. Ten years ago we made more radios and TVs than the rest of the world, and now you can't find a TV made in America."

I argue that competition for markets leads to wars, and that steel made by American, German, and Japanese steelworkers could end up being dropped on each other's cities.

"I'd like to see management stop the foremen from driving these little foreign cars," says Vandermeer, ignoring my remark. "Fletcher and the other general foreman, Downs, both drive Volkswagens. Marlowe drives a Toyota. It seems to me that anybody who depends on the steel industry for a paycheck should at least buy cars made from American steel. And then the way people fuck off around here. Go up on the casthouse, and what do you see? Half the crew asleep. When it's time to shovel the pit in the stockhouse, the laborers disappear, asleep somewhere, and the foreman's got to do it. That's why we're losing out."

The phone rings and Jackson answers. "South End." He hangs up and says, "That was the number three car man. His shoe came off the rail."

"I'll take this one," I answer. I am beginning to be able to respond to easy calls without Jackson, which of course lightens the workload for both of us. "How about taking my hand?" I say to Vandermeer.

"OK, but hurry back. I want to get a nap."

I give him my cards and get my tools out of the locker. As I go out the door, Jackson warns me, "Be careful. That rail is carrying 250 volts."

I go down to the stockhouse and climb up on the larry car. The collector shoe is a two-by-eight-by-eighteen-inch flat bar that pivots on the end of a four-foot metal arm. It rides along the hot (electrified) rail overhead, normally held in place by heavy spring pressure, as it transfers the electric current to the car. The shoe had burned up and would not stay on the rail. I get off the car and go over to the switchbox on the wall. I pull the breaker switch nearby to shut off the electricity. Then I get back on the car. I pull the shoe off the rail by means of the attached rope, then take the burnt shoe out of the arm assembly. In a storage box next to the breaker switch I find another shoe, which I put in place of the burnt one. Then I loosen the rope, allowing the spring to lift the shoe onto the rail, using the wooden handle of my hammer to position it. As soon as the shoe makes contact with the rail, the compressor motor on the car starts up and the car lights go on. My knees get weak; the rail has been energized all the time I worked next to it.

I get off the car and go to look at the breaker I thought I had shut off. I pulled the wrong switch! It controlled voltage to the highline. But because of its location, I assumed it fed the stockhouse hot rail. If I had touched the hot rail, I would have been fried like a potato chip.

When I get back to the shanty, Jackson and Sourwine are the only ones there. Szathmary had gone to help with a call on the North End, and Vandermeer had returned to his shanty to get some sleep and beat the Japanese. I tell Jackson and Sourwine what had happened.

"You were lucky you used your hammer to put that shoe back on the rail instead of your hand. You might have been fried," says Jackson.

"Lucky, hell," I reply, "I'm scared of that shit. I treat it like it's always hot."

"That's smart. If you're scared of it you're less likely to be hurt. It's the guys that ain't scared of electricity that get knocked on their ass."

"How about you? Ever been hurt?"

"If you work around this stuff long enough, you're bound to get bit. But I was only hurt once by electricity. I was working behind the skip board and my elbow must have brushed against something hot. I felt like I had been kicked by a mule. The stoveman, who was with me at the time, told me I got a dazed look on my face and sank to my knees. That was all. My arm was numb for a while. That was the only time I was hurt by electricity. I been hurt other times by things falling on me, getting my hand pinched, and stuff like that."

"There's a lot of ways to get hurt out here," Sourwine adds. "Remember last year when that guy was gassed on the North End? He almost died. He went up on top of the furnace while it was operating. There's gas all around there. He didn't have his gas mask, but he figured he could stand it for a minute. He was lucky that someone on his way down saw him passed out. He called the gas rescue crew, and they went up there with masks and carried him down."

"Yeah, I remember that," says Jackson. "They took him to the hospital and pumped oxygen into him for three hours, and then they tested him and found no traces of gas, so they put it down on the report as indigestion."

"I think that guy still acts weird," Sourwine replies. "This is a dangerous place. You got to look out for yourself, and you got to look out for everybody around you. Some people out here act like there aren't any safety rules. If people would follow the rules, there wouldn't be so many injuries."

42

"What do you mean?" I ask.

"They got an essjaypee for every operation out here. They're written down in a book in Fletcher's office. It tells how to perform every job safely, what to watch out for, and so on. That's what Szathmary reads to us from when we have a safety meeting."

"Give me an example of an essjaypee. How do you change cars safely in the stockhouse?"

"Well, first you're supposed to make sure that the track on both sides of you is clear. You're supposed to put track stops on the rails to stop the other cars from coming too close, or else post somebody with a flag to give warning."

"Do you do that when you're switching cars?"

"Most of the time the track stops are too far from where you need them, and they're too heavy to lug around. And even if you got a helper to post with a flag, most of the time he's off on another job somewhere or else asleep in the shanty."

"What else?"

"Well, you're supposed to make sure the switching track is free from obstructions so you won't get hurt throwing the switch."

"Do you do that?"

"Depends. A lot of times the switch is so fucked up with coke and ore and shit that you got to jump on it with both feet to budge it. If you try to get it cleaned, the foreman will tell you he hasn't got any laborers. If it's too bad I try to get the shit out with a pry bar."

"What else is there to the essjaypee?"

"Most of the rest is electrical. Jackson knows more about that than I do. Aren't you supposed to open the switch box to make sure the blades are out after you pull the switch?"

"That's right," says Jackson.

"Do we do that?" I ask.

"Not always. The doors on the boxes are so crudded up that you can skin your knuckles trying to get them open. Once in a while I'll check a box to make sure the blades are working right."

"How's the footing down there with all the pellets?"

"It says in the essjaypee," replies Sourwine, "that we're supposed to be alert and exercise caution when walking around pellets. They're really slippery and you can fall and break your ass on them."

I persist: "Do you think that is a safe way of working?"

"Yeah," Sourwine replies. "If people would only follow the procedure. The job is safe, but people don't follow it. It's as much my fault as anybody else's. I take short cuts, either because there's another job waiting or else because I want to get back to the shanty."

"So whose fault is it if a man slips and falls on the pellets?"

"His own, in most cases. If you're careful and take your time you won't fall on those things. It's just when you forget or start shooting the shit with the car man that you can get hurt."

"Let me ask you something," I say to Sourwine. "You own a house, don't you? If somebody falls and hurts himself on a crack in the sidewalk in front of your house, or slips on the ice, what will happen?"

"He'll sue. I'll be responsible."

"Suppose you pull out a written safe walking procedure that instructs passersby to exercise caution when walking on sidewalk cracks or over ice—would that protect you?"

"Of course not. They'd throw it out of court."

"Well, then, how come the company can get away with an ess-jaypee that puts the responsibility for an injury on the person who is hurt?"

"It doesn't really free them from responsibility. They'll still have to pay workman's compensation."

"The hell they will," Jackson interjects. "It doesn't work that way. If you get hurt the company will send somebody to your house and pick you up and bring you into the mill and give you a desk job—just so they don't have to pay comp. That's how they keep the accident rate down."

"Can they get away with that?"

"Shit, everybody knows that money talks," says Sourwine.

"What would happen if you followed all the safety rules exactly as they are written?"

"You couldn't get any work done," Jackson states. "You'd have to hold up the job waiting for them to get the equipment in shape before you touch it. You just watch sometime when you're in the skip house and the furnace is down. There can be a dozen blue hats in there, and if you're working on getting the furnace going they don't care if you're hopping on one leg. You can be without your glasses, without your hard hat — hell, you could be barefoot — but if they're in a hurry to get it running they won't even notice. But just you walk out of the shanty to take a piss without your hard hat on and some blue hat will come along and write you up for it."

"What if you get hurt rushing to get the job done?"

"It's your fault for failing to follow the essjaypee."

"So who does the essjaypee protect?"

"When you look at it that way," concludes Sourwine, "it does seem that the rules are there to protect the company, not the men."

I sit back, thinking I have accomplished enough for one night.

VIII

Months have passed since I started in the mill, and I am beginning to feel I know my way around. Shortly after I started as a motor inspector helper, the company announced that it was discontinuing the helper jobs, and all the helpers would either have to enter the apprentice program or take a layoff. I chose the former. But in order to do so I had to produce a copy of my high school diploma, which I didn't have. So I wrote to my high school, asking them to write to the Gary Works personnel office and assure them that I had, indeed, graduated high school. They wrote saying that I had finished near the top of my class and had won a prestigious scholarship. In short, they almost blew my cover. Fortunately, it did not set the personnel department's antennae to quivering, and I was able to enter the apprentice program.

In addition to producing my high school diploma, I had to take a test. It was the sort of aptitude test I was familiar with from college: Which word does not belong with the others, etc. I scored high on it. When the results came back the general foreman announced they had a genius among them, and I was given my choice of trades. I chose to remain with the motor inspectors, partly because I thought I would be happiest and be able to accomplish most in a gang with black workers, and partly because I liked working with Jackson. As an apprentice I attended school one day a week for four hours, learning about electricity and how to read blueprints. Once in the program, whatever academic skills I possessed were outweighed by the skills of my fellow apprentices. Most of them had grown up working on cars, boats, and tractors and doing plumbing and wiring around the house. As they were doing such things, I was learning to conjugate French verbs!

I worked for a few days with a black man about my age on a job that required some wire. I watched as the man reeled a length of wire from the spool three times as long as needed for the job. When I raised my eyebrows, the man said, "The people in the wire mills gotta have jobs, too." Whenever the boss called him he would always ask, "Who me?" I asked him why he always did that.

"Two reasons: the first is to give myself time to think what I might have screwed up so I can get my story ready. The second is, I figure it's to my advantage if he thinks I'm stupid. It means he expects less from me."

His attitude contrasted with mine. In spite of my politics, I was never able to achieve a total separation from bourgeois values. Of all the things that offended me about my supervisors, probably the one that most got under my skin was being thought stupid. That attitude was a legacy of my class background.

For some time, the majority of the people in Gary, Indiana, where the mill was located, were black. In 1967 they were able to oust the old white political machine and elect a black mayor, Richard Hatcher. Gary was among the first cities in the country to do so. Just before I started in the mill in 1972, Gary hosted the National Black Political Convention, which was attended by prominent black figures ranging from liberal to radical. Mayor Hatcher delivered the opening address, declaring that the black movement was a progressive force that could transform the country and carry the "best of the whites" along with it. STO reprinted and circulated his speech.

For my first six months in the mill I commuted from Chicago. Entering the apprenticeship program brought with it a modest degree of job security, and I decided it was time to move closer to the mill. Most whites who worked in the mill lived in surrounding all-white towns. There are still areas of the city that are majority white, but the residents are mainly middle-class and professional, largely Jewish. One of the predominately white districts, Miller Beach, had once been an independent town. Many of its residents still regarded themselves as Miller Beach residents, rather than part of Gary. This made them a target of ridicule by the city's black residents. Miller Beach had its own shopping mall, which the black residents of Gary refused to patronize.

I made a small down payment on a home in a black area, a two-bedroom brick with a small fenced yard, on the east, or poorer, side of town, a mile-and-a-half from the gate where I normally enter work. I also acquired a dog from the local shelter, a Spaniel mixed-breed puppy, who I named Swee'Pea. I considered adopting a local dog as another sign of my commitment to integrating myself with the industry, the mill, and Gary's residents. On my days off I walked Swee'Pea along the dunes on the lakefront nearby, within sight of the mill.

Jackson is a strong bridge player. He teaches me to play. And soon we begin going regularly to bridge evenings. Aside from enjoying these evenings, the club offered me a window into black life, revealing to me the fluid nature of class in the black community. Like most social activities in Gary, card playing was segregated by race. Whist and bridge are similar, but bridge was regarded as more elevated. Whist, or "negro bridge," is popular among black people; only a minority among them played bridge. The club we attended catered to the black "middle class" of the town—mainly school teachers and social workers, but it also included the wife of the newly-elected black mayor, and another maintenance worker from the mill who was having an affair with the wife of a doctor. I was ordinarily the only non-black participant. Jackson and I played as a team, and normally did well, owing largely to Jackson's skill. One time we went to Chicago and played in a tournament in the "white" league, and finished near the top.

After moving to Gary I decide to hold a party in my new home and invite many of my fellow workers. It may have been one of the only racially integrated working-class social events in the town. I wonder if I should invite Szathmary, who I like and who is generally popular among the men. Years earlier, when Szathmary and his cohort were coming up and before they made foreman, they assigned each other feline nicknames: Szathmary was Little Cat. (Red, the hardass, was Polecat.) In the factories where I had worked previously, workers and foremen did not interact socially. I wasn't sure whether this applied in the mill. On one hand, foremen frequently did physical labor alongside the men. Also, management had made clear how little they thought of the foremen by discharging dozens on a single day, known by them as "Black Friday" (which they were powerless to resist, since they were not union members). On the other hand, they had a certain authority and power of discipline over the men. I was concerned that Szathmary's feelings would be hurt if he was not invited. I asked Jackson what he thought.

"He's never invited me to his home," was the reply. That settled it, so far as I was concerned.

IX

Autumn, and our crew is now working four-to-twelve. We decide it is time to go fishing. Jackson tells us that he knows a pond not too far away that is full of lake perch, which make for great eating, especially when cooked in butter. Jackson and I are both avid fishermen. Szathmary had given it up, but he knows a lot about it. Sourwine doesn't know much, but is interested. Slick doesn't know and doesn't want to know.

"I'm a city boy. The only kind of fish I want to see is the kind laying on ice in the market. The rest is just mosquitoes, snakes, and poison ivy."

Jackson says, "We can get to the pond in a couple of hours. If we leave when we get off, we could be there before the sun comes up, waiting for the fish to start biting."

"I've got an outboard motor," I tell him, "a seven-and-a-half-horse that cost me twenty-five bucks. It used to work but doesn't anymore, and I can't find a place to get it fixed on account of it's an old model they quit making."

"I'll bet we could fix it out here," says Sourwine. "We got the tools, and all of us working on it together could do it. If only there was a way of getting it into the mill. I don't think the guards would let you carry it in on your back."

All eyes turn toward Szathmary, who has a new red Ford pickup truck and who, as a foreman, is permitted to drive into the mill. He agrees to help out. After he leaves on an errand, I ask if foremen ever take advantage of their drive-in privilege to help themselves to the company's equipment and material. Jackson tells us about one foreman who stole so much that by the time the company caught and fired him, he had accumulated enough money to buy a liquor store.

The conversation soon expands to the general topic of pilfering from the mill. Legends abounded: one story of a guy who told the foreman he needed a three-foot length of copper wire for a job at home, and asked him for a pass. The foreman gave him a pass saying, "Pass Joe with wire," upon which Joe walked out with a three-hundred-yard spool. Another story is of a guy who wrapped copper sheeting around himself under his overcoat. All went well until he tripped and fell by the guard shack and found himself rocking back and forth on his back like a turtle, unable to stand. Then there was the one of the guy who every day would exit the plant gate with a wheelbarrow covered by a tarpaulin. The guard would dutifully lift the tarp and, seeing nothing under it, would pass the man through. At the man's retirement the guard asked him,

"C'mon, man, you can tell me now. I know you were stealing all those years. What was it?"

"Wheelbarrows!"

The following afternoon, I meet Szathmary outside the gate and load the motor onto the back of his truck, covering it with a tarpaulin. When Szathmary comes to the shanty later, we heave the motor off and clamp it to the rim of an empty fifty-gallon oil drum, its propeller inside. We start it up and watch it emit smoke without causing the propeller to rotate. We then lift it out of the drum and set it on a table.

All five of us work together to disassemble the motor, examining the various parts for defects. Sourwine's hands and forehead are quickly streaked with grease. At last we find the trouble; a rubber fitting has rotted. Szathmary says he knows where there was a sheet of hard rubber from which we could make a replacement for the damaged part. While he goes off to retrieve it, I put on a second pot of coffee.

Suddenly the door opens and Greene, the general foreman, enters. He greets everyone and sits down on the bench.

"Deal 'em out, men. I've got a busy night and I want to get in a few hands before all hell breaks loose."

"What's the matter with you, Greene?" asks Jackson. "Can't you see we're working?" He points at the motor on the table.

Greene goes over and peers at the motor. "Whose is this?"

"We're waiting for Szathmary to get back with a part so we can put it back together," says Jackson, avoiding Greene's question.

"I guess I'll wait, then. If there's one thing I hate to do, it's to interfere with steel men in the performance of their duties."

"With that kind of devotion you could go far around here," Slick responds.

"The brothers-in-law that run things don't appreciate it," says Greene, returning to his favorite topic. "Did you see their latest brilliant project, up there on the side of number one?"

"What's it supposed to be?" asks Sourwine.

"Where you guys been the last ten years? It's going to be a 'smiley,'—you know, one of those circles with lines for the eyes and mouth."

"What they putting that up for?"

"It's part of the campaign this guy Hemple brought with him from Pittsburgh. When it's finished it'll say 'Have a safe work day.' They think it will raise morale and lower the accident rate."

Slick throws his hands in the air. "I've been here a long time and that's about the best I've seen. A 'smiley' on the side of a fuckin' blast furnace. How much did that bright idea cost?"

"Well, I didn't see the exact figures, but talk is that the final cost will come to more than eight thousand dollars, a lot of it for overtime."

"Ain't that a bitch," says Slick.

Szathmary comes into the shanty, carrying a piece of rubber about one-quarter of an inch thick and two feet square.

"This ought to do it." And taking out his pocket knife with the curved blade he carefully cuts out a small piece of rubber the size of the one that had rotted away. Then he drives a hole in it with a hammer and punch. Comparing it with the original he nods with satisfaction and begins to reassemble the motor.

When we finish we set the motor back in the barrel and pull the cord to start it up. It runs smoothly, without emitting a cloud of smoke.

"OK, load it on my truck and we'll get it out of here."

Jackson and I carry the motor out and put it in the bed of Szathmary's truck. At the end of our shift it will be transferred back to my car outside the gate. We then return to the shanty. Szathmary leaves to drive up to the North End to check on the crew there. Jackson goes to the sink to wash his hands while I begin wiping the oil off the work table with an old rag.

Meanwhile, Greene, who was impatient to get in some card-playing, has cleared the makeshift card table and dealt out four hands. He is sitting alone, waiting for the others to join him.

"Just a minute, Greene," says Sourwine. "Wait 'til I pour this cup of coffee."

This scene will always stick with me in perfect clarity, as in a film where motion is frozen at the moment of impact: me wiping off the work table, Jackson at the sink, Sourwine pouring coffee, Slick sitting at the far end of the bench cleaning his tools — and Greene sitting by himself at the card table with four hands dealt out in front of him.

Nothing in the events reported so far is particularly special. With slight variations the scene has occurred hundreds of times. What makes this scene memorable is what happens next. Just at that moment of this unforgettable scene, the door opens and in walks Hemple, the plenipotentiary from company headquarters in Pittsburgh who is charged with eliminating waste and getting things moving.

It would have been serious if he had surprised all of us playing cards on Company time. It would have been still more serious if he had come across three workers and a shift foreman so occupied. But to walk in on the general foreman of the South End of the blast furnace division of the largest works of the largest steel company sitting at a table by himself with four hands dealt out in front of him — one can only imagine the reaction of an executive who takes his work so seriously that he orders the painting of a smiley-face on the side of a blast furnace.

Nobody utters a sound. Greene frantically tries to scoop up the cards. Realizing the futility of his efforts, he looks up at Hemple, a sickly smile on his face, which by this time has paled dangerously and is showing signs of the tint represented in his name. Hemple storms out of the shanty; Greene, like a sheep being led to its shearing, follows him. A moment later he walks back in, sheepishly, as the words "safety violation" can be heard outside, to retrieve the hard hat he had forgotten in his haste.

Later that evening, when Szathmary returns from the North End he inquires of Greene's whereabouts.

"I thought he was going to play some dirty hearts."

"He couldn't stay," explains Jackson. "Sit down and take a hand. We need a fourth."

The night before our last turn, we tell Szathmary not to bring his lunch the next night. We will feed everyone fresh perch!

We set off shortly after midnight, with our tackle in the trunks of our cars and the worms we had purchased at a bait shop the previous afternoon in a cooler along with an ample supply of beer. We leave the city and drive out to the pond in the next county, arriving three hours before sunup, and set up. All the books and experts plus our own experience assure us it is the best time to fish. Alas, the fish didn't read the books or listen to the experts. We fish steadily until the sun comes up and a few hours beyond. Between the three of us, we catch only a single bluegill.

"I guess that's why they call it 'fishing' instead of 'catching,'" says Jackson.

"What do we do now?" I ask. "We can't go in tonight empty-handed."

"I know a fish market not far away," says Sourwine, who lives in the town nearby. "We can go by there and get some perch and take them in with us. Nobody will know the difference."

Jackson and I readily agree. We really have no other choice.

"But let's make sure the guy at the market doesn't gut or scale them," I say.

We arrive at the mill the next afternoon with our "catch" in a cooler, along with the butter, potatoes, and everything else we need. Jackson reports that the fish were biting so hard we had to hide behind trees to bait our hooks. All the men help gut and scale the fish and peel the potatoes. I cook the meal in a twelve-inch cast-iron skillet on the little hot plate, dredging the fish in a mix of flour and cornmeal with salt and pepper. Everyone enjoys the feast—there is enough for the crew and a little extra for some of the carmen—and if anyone caught on to the deception, nobody says anything.

X

I am having a hard time adjusting to the weekly rotation. Just as I got so I could sleep during the day, it's time to go back to working days and sleeping nights. I feel as if my body is operating with several cylinders missing.

On one occasion I am called out to repair a pump. In order to reach it, I have to enter a dark space through a five-foot-high opening. Going from the bright light to the dark, I bump my hard hat against the low door. The hat jams into my safety glasses, which in turn dig into my eye socket beneath the eyebrow, opening up a cut. They take me to the infirmary and stitch me up. Since this happens near the end of my shift, they let me go home.

The next night back in the shanty Szathmary has a meeting of the crew. Reading from the essjaypee book, he points out where it says people should use caution before entering areas that are not well lit. I protest.

"It seems to me that the door is too low. How can they expect a man to duck every time he has to go through a low door, especially when the light's against him?"

I refuse to sign the report assigning me the blame. Szathmary must have been convinced by my argument, because when he writes up the report, he attributes the injury to the door being too low. It is the first time within living memory that an injury had been written up as the company's fault.

"I'll leave instructions for the welders to burn the openings higher," Szathmary states.

Of course that is not what happened; In the usual company way, instead of cutting the doorways higher so that a person of my height can pass through without hitting his head, they send maintenance workers around with rolls of fluorescent diagonally-striped tape that they fasten over low doors. The tape strips became known as "Noel's sticky tape."

The valves on the stoves that control the blasts of air into the furnace open in sequence, one closing before the next one opens. Because they are operated automatically, each valve has a switch that indicates when it is closed, completing the circuit that signals to the next valve that it is safe to open. However, on one of the furnaces they have installed a drinking fountain, right above one of the switches, that runs continuously. Most of the time this isn't a problem. The water overflows the bowl and drips onto the valve, but it doesn't seem to interfere with the operation of the switch. However... when winter comes and the temperature falls, the dripping water freezes on the switch, preventing it from registering closed and sending a false signal that prevents the next valve from opening.

Then the stove man calls over the PA:

"MOTOR INSPECTOR, VALVE WON'T OPEN ON NUMBER THREE. VALVE WON'T OPEN ON NUMBER THREE."

When that call comes either Jackson or I have to go out and inspect the valve visually to make sure that it is closed and set up the signal for the next valve to open. Having verified that everything is OK and that the frozen switch is giving a false reading, we would climb up on a railing, beat the icicles off the switch with a hammer, and jiggle it manually to complete the circuit.

That gets old pretty quickly—especially when it happens three or four times in the course of a single midnight shift when we are trying to get a little sleep and the temperature is ten below. On those occasions we are tempted to bypass the switch, which we can do from the circuit board in the skip house, without exposing ourselves to the cold.

"What would happen if we did that and the valve wasn't really closed and the next one opened?" I ask Jackson.

"You could kiss the northwest corner of Indiana goodbye, and your ass with it," explains Jackson.

I think about that exchange years later when I am touring a nuclear power plant. One of the things I observe there is a ten-foot long platform made of wooden planks which some ingenious soul has stretched over two railings.

"That's where the maintenance workers on the midnight shift sleep," I am thinking. And visions of Three Mile Island and Chernobyl came into my mind.

It is January. Gary Works is situated on the southern tip of Lake Michigan with hardly a single elevation to break the wind between it and the North Pole. Working out-of-doors much of the time, we feel the cold to our bones, no matter how many layers of silk, wool, and down we wear. One night Red, the foreman, and I are making a repair at the top of the rafters in a barn open to the weather where rail cars were repaired. It is 3 a.m., and connecting the wires requires us to remove our gloves — although it is a toss-up on whether we gain or lose more dexterity by working bare-handed. I am so cold tears form in my eyes. I am tempted to go home. Why should I freeze my ass for U.S. Steel? But the thought that if I leave, Red, the old man, would have to finish the job alone stopped me. I feel grateful to the mornings I spent delivering papers with my father twenty years earlier, when as a point of pride, we refused gloves even on the coldest days.

There is no sleeping or playing cards on day turns. In the intervals between calls I often find myself getting restless and squirming around on the hard bench while the time drags on. Nevertheless I find myself looking forward to these periods because they give me the chance to catch up on the happenings from the maintenance workers who work straight days instead of shift work.

There is a constant battle between management and the day gang over shanty time. The men are expected to go to the shanty in the morning, pick up their tools, and go out on the job they had been assigned that day, returning only for a half-hour lunch and later at quitting time to put away their tools. However, they stretch their time in the shanty as much as they can. They have coffee in the morning after line-up, return to the shanty as much as a half-hour before lunch, and come in early in the afternoon to wash up and put away their tools. During the day they often drop into the shanty, ostensibly to get parts for the job from their lockers, taking advantage of the errand to relax. Often, even at times when Jackson and I are the only ones officially allowed in the shanty, it is full, with millwrights, motor inspectors, and other maintenance people from the day shift, and even laborers taking a break. One time I answered the phone when the general foreman called the shanty looking for one of the day crew. Even though the man was there, I say he is out on a job. This won me the appreciation of the man himself and others on the day crew. Occasionally one or another foreman from the front office would raid the shanty before lunch, chasing out those who were not authorized to be there, and for a few days it would be relatively empty before things gradually return to normal.

Many of the men are from rural backgrounds. The Americans from the South, black or white, talk about corn and cotton, fishing, hunting, and dogs. The Poles talk about growing cabbage, the Greeks about olives. One night I accompany a Greek immigrant up to the rafters of a repair barn, where we gather nesting pigeons which the man insists are a delicacy. He recounted how he had gathered them back home, and shows me how to pluck their feathers and cook them. After some initial reluctance, I try them and find them tasty.

Among the members of the day gang are Stokes and White. They are both black men, and avowed Christians. Stokes is a welder; White had been a turn motor inspector but had been forced to drop down to a lower-paying job because he refused to work Sundays. He regards Sunday work as a violation of the Sabbath. Belonging to different denominations, they often hold extended discussions over doctrine, citing passages from the Bible as evidence. Their disputes about the all-loving, all-merciful, and all-forgiving God often got so heated that each appears ready to murder the other. When they get too noisy, others in the shanty tell them to shut up, pipe down, etc.

One day Stokes turns to me and asks, "How about you, brother—have you found Christ?"

"Why, is he lost?" I joke.

"No, but you are if you haven't found Him."

"I don't want to be unfriendly, but I expect you'll have more success arguing with Brother White than with me."

Before Stokes can pursue this further, White calls Stokes over excitedly to show him a verse he had found that demonstrated the soundness of his interpretation of Bible law. They soon have their heads buried in the book.

Sourwine is sitting next to me. I ask: "What do you think about all of this?"

"As far as I'm concerned," he answers, "if I can't see it, feel it, taste it, smell it, or fuck it, it doesn't exist."

There is no shortage of characters at the mill. One fellow has written a book, with maps and charts, "proving" that the earth is shaped like an apple with a bite out of one side, and that flying saucers are visitors from the "bite." The odd thing is that his understanding of global geography does not seem to affect his life in any practical way. For example, he always seems to know what route to take to Detroit and how long it takes to get there.

Another man has a theory that a superior species has conquered the earth and is raising all of us for food. "What else can explain the world?" he would inquire of doubters in a perfectly reasonable tone. Other than on that one subject, he, too, seems unaffected by his bizarre view.

One fellow thinks weather forecasters deliberately exaggerate the severity of upcoming storms in order to sell more snowblowing machines. No one argues with him.

Another always walks around with a paperback book in his pocket, and takes every opportunity to take it out and read it. Curiosity gets the better of me and I ask him what he's reading. It is a pornographic pulp that he reads over and over. The discovery makes me feel unclean, and now I make sure not to sit too close to him on the bench.

One day the men were kidding around. I suggest they need more exalted job descriptions. I give myself a new title, "Electrical diagnostic technician," and attach it to my hard hat.

Dust from the furnace is collected by a dust catcher where it is wetted and transferred to wagons and stored in special tanks. The job of cleaning the tanks normally fell on the millwrights. It is a particularly dirty job. The person assigned the job follows my example and puts his new title, "Particle emissions technician," on his hard hat. Several other maintenance workers do the same, modifying their titles as appropriate.

One of the older motor inspectors, troubleshooting an electric circuit, replaces the fuse with a solid copper bar able to withstand the highest current and then turns the power all the way up. The pipe blackens and gives off smoke through the insulation. Now he knows there is a problem. He never does this in the presence of supervisors.

One man shares an article from the local newspaper about the high levels of pollution in another steel town.

"I don't know how those people can live like that," he says, as tiny particles from the blast furnace rain down on him. When he wakes in the morning, he tells us that his pillow is the color of rust!

One of my favorite characters is Poulos, who I worked with my first two days in the mill. Poulos is so consistently sour in his outlook and so narrow in his interests that he fascinates me. For the last two years he has been the highest-seniority motor inspector in the blast furnace division. That distinction brings with it privileges, among which is his regular job in the skip house. It is a soft job, consisting to a large extent of waiting around for the furnace to fill up so he can stop the skip and work on the control board. In good weather he spends most of his waiting time leaning on the rail on the walkway outside the skip house, watching the traffic up and down the furnace road. The common sight of him leaning on the rail stimulates comments.

"Been polishing the rail?" says one man, as the day crew is washing up for lunch. The man is a few years younger than I.

"Why, you puppy, be quiet when the men are talking. You haven't started to lift your leg when you pee. I've got more time in the shanty than you've got in the mill. I've got more time getting my ass chewed out in Fletcher's office than you've got in the mill."

Poulos talks as if everything around him was put there to make him unhappy. Supervisors, co-workers and helpers, auto and TV repairmen, traffic cops and parking lot attendants, telephone operators and bus drivers—all make his life difficult, and he wages the struggle against them with unflagging energy.

Today he is complaining about the trash collection. In Gary where he lives, and where the mill is located, residents have elected a black mayor following a series of white crooks and incompetents. But he claims that his trash is not being picked up as often as before.

"They used to come twice a week. If they missed a day I could call City Hall and they'd send a truck. Now it sits for a week."

Jackson, who takes special pleasure in needling Poulos, responds, "That's how it works. It used to be my trash would be there in the alley. Now I can call City Hall and they'll send a truck right away. It shouldn't bother you, though—white trash doesn't smell as bad as black trash."

Poulos sneers at him and shifts to complaining about his neighbor, with whom he has been battling ever since he moved onto the block.

"The son of a bitch. He lets his dog shit on the bushes in front of my house. He parks his car in front of my house. Who the hell wants a ten-year-old Chevy that hasn't been washed since he bought it sitting in front of his house? Use common sense, Jackson. Would you want it? This morning I came out and found a pile of cigarette butts on my curb. The son of a bitch emptied the ashtray from his car."

"You need to move to the ghetto," Jackson replies. "We like to throw our trash out the second-story window. It helps the grass grow."

"I told the son of a bitch," continues Poulos, "to quit dirtying up my curb or I was gonna get the law on him. He just laughs in my face. He said if he felt like it he would come over and take a shit on my front doorstep and there wasn't a thing I could do about it."

The men are laughing (except Poulos). Jackson, holding his sides, asks, "What did you tell him?"

"I told him if he ever shit on my doorstep it would be the undertaker that wiped his ass."

"Hey, Poulos," says Jackson, "Tell us about the time you worked foreman in the stockhouse."

"Up yours."

"I heard it from the car man. Poulos wrote out the sheet wrong and had him send up twenty-seven skip loads of limestone in a row. There was so much stone in the furnace they were casting bricks."

"I suppose you never made a mistake in your life, huh? I suppose you're one of those geniuses like Fletcher. I feel sorry for you, kid, having to work helper with a genius like Jackson."

The laughter is cut off by the ring of the telephone. Since it is a full half-hour before lunchtime, everyone falls silent in case it's the office calling.

I answer the phone, listen, say OK, and hang up. That was number five car man. His skip has stopped."

"Want to try this one by yourself?" asks Jackson. "Let's see how much you know."

I grab my tools and go up to the skip house. The giant motors are still; the skip cables won't move. I look at the control board covered with what seems to me a thousand relays, each looking like all the others. I walk over and push one of them with my hammer handle, as I have seen Jackson do. Nothing happens. I push another, and the skip moves a few feet, stopping with a loud crash of the brakes. Holding one relay in with the hammer handle, I push another with my flashlight. This time there is a big blast of air, as one of the giant bells on the furnace top falls and rises.

The car man on number five calls over the PA, "BLOWER ON FIVE CAN'T FILL. SKIP STOP ON NUMBER FIVE."

I am beginning to get rattled. I push another relay, which makes three more move in sequence, but still the skip doesn't move. I try it again. Both bells open slowly at the same time and I hear the sound of coal particles falling on the corrugated roof of the skip house.

As I am standing there staring at the board, the blower walks in.

"Don't you think you had better call the motor inspector?" he asks.

I pick up the phone on the wall and call the shanty. When Jackson answers, I say, "I think you'd better come up here."

Number five is close to the shanty, so it is less than a minute before Jackson appears at the door. To me it seems like an hour with the blower watching me.

It takes Jackson only a minute to straighten out the mess on the skip board and start the skip on its travel. We stand there and watch it make several trips, while Jackson explains the operation.

After the blower leaves the skip house, Jackson says, "Let me give you some advice. If you get in trouble up here, or anyplace else, don't ever lie to Szathmary. He'll see right through you. And don't ever tell the truth to the blower or any of these production foremen."

"What'll I tell them?"

"Tell them anything. Make up something. Tell them about differential harmonic imbalance or some other bullshit, or tell them you need parts from the shanty, and call me. They don't know anything about these furnaces and will believe anything you say. Just don't let them see you're in trouble."

I resolve to keep the advice in mind. When we get back to the shanty we pour ourselves coffee and sit down. The door bursts open and a man of about forty with the label "natural gas" on the front of his hard hat enters. He begins to sing:

"I'm just a plain old country boy, a cornbread lovin' country boy, I raise hell on Saturday night, but I go to church on Sunday."

Turning around, he points a finger at Jackson.

"Every time the preacher come, Ma would fix some chicken. If I reached for the drumstick I was sure to get a lickin'. I'd take the part she gave me and I'd better shut my mouth—The gizzard and the north end of a chicken heading south.

His accent leaves no doubt he is from the South.

"How you doing, country boy" asked Jackson.

"Who are you callin' 'boy?' Have you ever tried on my shoes? I didn't get in 'til four this morning. My old lady asked what I was doing coming home at that hour. I told her it was the only place open. If my mother knew where I was and how I was doing, she'd send the mule out to bring me home. Can I have some of your coffee?

"Get yourself a cup from the locker," says Jackson. "The white one is the pussy-eaters' cup."

"Just so it's white. Hey, boy, you're the new helper, huh? He's not bad to work with, for a darky. My name's Thurman." He sticks out his hand, which I shake.

I consider asking about the "natural gas" label, which Thurman had peeled off one of the pipes on the furnace floor, but decide not to out of fear that Thurman would demonstrate the reason.

Thurman is a machinist. More exactly, he is a member of the machinists' gang. Machinists in the mill are unlike any I have seen in other shops. In the first place, they spend more time away from the lathes, drill presses, and milling machines than they do with them. Most of their work is in the field mounting motors, gears, and other equipment. In the second place, their methods would horrify anyone familiar with standard machining practices. On one occasion I watched two of the machinists putting a large steel gear on a shaft over a brass bushing. The gear refused to slide on and, instead of applying the lubricating grease ordinarily used in such situations, or polishing the bushing with emery cloth, they simply picked up a sledge hammer and pounded it on, an act which would have got them summarily fired from any self-respecting machine shop. Having worked in machine shops, I was forced to turn my head away when this happened.

Of all the machinists in the blast furnace division of the largest works of U.S. Steel, Thurman stands out. His name was a synonym for doing the job wrong. That is, he makes so many mistakes in machining the parts or assembling them in the field, the other machinists, when they ruined a piece, would say they had "Thurmaned" it.

The maintenance foremen dealt with Thurman's tendency to screw up any job by not giving him any jobs to do. When lining up the crew in the morning they would assign him to inspect valve covers—something they were reasonably confident he could do without causing damage—and then leaving him alone. Another job they liked to give him was removing broken screws from brackets. Some of the workers had divided his yearly earnings by the number of broken screws he had removed from brackets and calculated that it cost U.S. Steel two hundred fifty-seven dollars and thirty-two cents for every screw.

On payday a foreman commented to Thurman, "Well, you milked U.S. Steel another week."

"After you foremen get all the cream, there's nothing left for us but milk," was the reply.

Thurman doesn't mind his peculiar job assignments; they fit in with his life, which is to drink and party all night long and then come to work in the morning to sleep. He is the acknowledged leader in shanty time; often he spends the whole day going from one shanty to another, sleeping a bit in each. In this way he recovers his strength for another night's carousing.

"So there I was," he recounts, "leaning back on a chair in the North End maintenance shanty with my hat tilted down and my feet up on a bench. I must have been snoring. The next thing I know, this new guy from Pittsburgh—what's-his-name Humple or Hemple or something—is standing there looking at me. So I wink at him. He looks at me some more, and asks me what I was doing."

"'I'm just sitting here tryin' to figure out how to get your job,' I tell him. He just stomped out of the shanty."

Thurman finishes his coffee and leaves, to "take a break," as he put it. When he had gone, I asked Jackson what he thinks of the "boy" and "darky" talk.

"One thing about Thurman, I know where he stands. With some people it's hard to tell."

XI

When I get to the shanty for the start of my series of four-to-twelve turns, I find an unfamiliar face. Jackson introduces him.

"This is Slick. He's replacing Vandermeer as the millwright."

Slick is a dark skinned black man of medium height and slight build. He and I shake hands.

He is telling a story of woe that had befallen an old friend.

"This old guy I know in town, an old German machinist, one of those quiet guys that gets along with everybody—came here after the War and got himself a job in a machine shop and worked there for years and saved his money for retirement. Last year he retired and took his savings and bought the thing he had always wanted—a new Mercedes diesel. This guy and his wife had been split up for a couple of years, but they weren't divorced. So to keep her from getting the car, he puts it in his girlfriend's name. Well, three months later, the bitch put him out on the street and kept the car."

The listeners emitted groans of pain.

"It's funny," says Slick. "When I tell that story to women they laugh and slap their knees."

"It's hard to please women," says Sourwine. "I bought my wife a new washing machine for our anniversary, and it didn't make her the least bit happy."

"Why should it?" says Slick. "That's her job. How would you feel if she bought you a new pipewrench?"

"Women can be cold," replies Sourwine. "I worked with this guy—he's not here anymore. His wife divorced him, and when her lawyer was done with him he owed money on the clothes he was wearing. He said if he ever needed a lawyer he would hire that one. Anyhow, the alimony was killing him, and he figured the best thing to do was to get her married again. You know, a man's best friend is the one who makes his ex-wife happy. So he used to bring guys from the job over to his ex-wife's house and introduce them. Well, she finally hit it off with one of the guys and they began dating. Then the guy moved in with her, and it looked like it was just a matter of time before they got married and his worries would be over. But then the guy that was living with her lost his job. They couldn't get married if he was out of work, but she liked him, so she let him stay. Do you know he stayed there for two years without working, living off the checks the ex was sending? If that ain't cold, tell me what is."

"Seems to me the fool got what he deserved, trying to pass off that bad news to his buddy," says Slick.

"Anyone know stories where the man wins?" I ask.

"Here's one," says Slick. "These two guys worked together, were real close friends. One payday, one of the guys had to work over, so he asked his friend to cash his paycheck and carry the money to his wife, who needed it for groceries. See, that's how close they were—they could trust each other with their pay. So the guy cashed the check and was on his way over to his buddy's house and he got to thinking. When he got there he didn't say anything about the money, just told the woman that her husband had to work over. She thanked him and invited him in for a cup of coffee. While they were sitting there, he offered her fifteen dollars for a kiss. She thought to herself, what's a kiss, and she could use the fifteen bucks, so she kissed him. He liked it, and after that had another cup of coffee and then asked her to go to bed with him for two hundred and fifty. That's as much as my husband brings home, she thought, and what the heck no one will be any the worse off. So they did the thing, and when they were done the guy left the two-fifty. That afternoon, when her husband got home he asked if his buddy had been by with the money. She looked at him. 'Yeah, he was by,' she said."

"You call that winning?" says Sourwine. "That's not what I call it. What about the husband? Did he win?"

"He didn't lose," says Slick. "What he didn't know didn't hurt him. It ain't like soap, you know. It don't wear out."

"Some women need a beating sometimes. It seems like they beg for it," says Sourwine, whom no one could imagine as a wife-beater.

"When I was a kid," I say, "my old man told us never to hit a man with glasses or a woman with a baby in her arms. My brother thought about that for a minute and asked, 'What about a woman with glasses?'"

"Some women are bigger than you are, and they'll deck you in a minute if you let 'em." It is Jackson's turn. "Back home in Missouri, when I was a youngster, I took this girl to a party. She was in her teens, same as me. Before the night ended I got rough with her. Over the next few days I heard that her daddy had found out about it and was so mad nobody could tell for sure what would happen if we ever met.

"It was a small town, and I knew I couldn't avoid him for long, so I figured I might as well face the music. So I went to his home and knocked on the door. The old man answered and when he saw who it was he was so mad he started to tremble. I knew I didn't have much time, so I started right in. I said to him, 'Sir, I know you are angry because you heard I got rough with your daughter, but before you do anything I want you to hear my side.'

"He was a fair man, and he waited for me to go on. 'Before we went out you told me that you were trusting your daughter to me, that I was responsible for her safety while she was with me, and that you expected me to have her back by eleven. Well, sir, I accepted that responsibility. We went to the party, just as we said, and while we were there she began to dance with a lot of the fellows. We were all having a good time. When I told her it was time for us to be going, she said she wanted one of the other fellows to take her home.'

"'I told her I didn't mind who she went out with any other night, but tonight she went out with me and she wasn't going home with anybody else.

"'She didn't like that idea, and started to holler and carry on. I grabbed her by the arm and dragged her out. That is my story, and if you are still mad, well, here I am.'

"When I finished talking the old man looked at me and said, 'You are right, son, and I am sorry I got angry with you. You were just doing what I asked you to do.'

"We shook hands and I left."

When I came in I noticed that one-third of the immense wall of number one furnace is covered with bright blue paint. I ask if anybody knows why.

"You never can tell with anything in this place," growls Slick. He has the deepest, coarsest voice of anyone I have ever met. His voice reflects numberless cigarettes and glasses of whiskey. No one calls him by the name he was given at birth, Bernard.

"I been here twenty-three years, though, and this is the first time I ever saw them paint a blast furnace.

"If you don't mind me asking, how did you get into the mill?" I ask.

"I didn't choose this place as a career, I can tell you. Very few people here did. I had to leave Detroit in a hurry due to a mixup with the law. I was heading for the Coast and decided to stop off for a few weeks to accumulate a stake. That was twenty-three years, a wife, and two kids ago."

"How'd you get to be called Slick?" I ask.

"Why you think?"

He was a sharp dresser, preferring expensive clothes of good fabric and conservative cut. Wide reading had given him the ability to talk with everyone from the dice-roller to the professor of comparative literature. Marriage had not slowed down his womanizing, nor diminished his appreciation for the comic side of the battle of the sexes. He gave all his girlfriends men's nicknames so his wife wouldn't know who he was talking to in case he slipped while talking to one of them on the phone. He routinely referred to women as "bitches," as in "So the bitch said..." His teenage daughter used to warn visiting friends, "Sooner or later, my father is going to slip and call you a bitch. Just be ready."

Once, out of a sense of duty, I remonstrated with him. Slick laughs it off. Not wishing to be thought priggish, I do not pursue the matter.

The phone rings and Jackson picks up. "South End."

It is a call from number six. I get my tools from the locker and go out the door. It is an easy call, just changing a light bulb on the cord used by the casthouse crew. The only reason they call me is that they don't have the tool to remove a broken bulb from its socket. When I get back to the shanty, Jackson is gone. Sourwine says he has gone out to answer another call. The three men are drinking coffee when Jackson returns.

"Gentlemen," Jackson says excitedly when he opens the door, "Good times are here. I was just over by the fish trap and it's full of smelt, just flopping around, waiting to be eaten."

"What's the fish trap?" I ask.

"They got a setup to strain fish out of the water they pull in from the lake. The outlet is over behind number six. When the smelt are running they pull in hundreds of them. They come out a pipe and fall into a big bucket, still flopping around. You can go over and pick them up, as many as you can eat."

The door opens and Szathmary came in. Jackson tells him the news.

"I thought it was getting to be that time of year," says the foreman. "What do you say fellows, do you think it's time for a feast?"

The response is enthusiastic. The crew then begins making plans for the fish fry, that will take place the following night. We agree who will bring the cooking oil, the bread, the salt and pepper and the flour and potatoes needed for a first-class meal of fried smelt. We agree that Szathmary will cook. He goes to his locker, extracting two good-sized cast-iron skillets.

"These ought to do the job."

The following evening, Jackson, Sourwine, Slick, and I all show up early, in high spirits with appetites, to relieve the day shift. We have work to do for the first part of the evening: the motor inspectors fix up the casthouses with lights, answer a few stove calls and start a stalled skip; the millwrights tighten the breaks on a few of the stockhouse cars according to the wishes of their operators.

Around six, after the day crew has gone home and when things seem to be settling down a bit, Szathmary asked, "Well, what do you think? Does it look about time?"

Sourwine sets up the card table, which tonight will serve as the dining-hall table. Jackson picks up a bucket and goes out the door toward the fish trap. Slick washes and dries the skillets. I begin peeling and slicing potatoes. Szathmary puts the skillets on the hotplate and pours oil into them. He puts the sliced potatoes into one.

Jackson returns with the bucket full of smelt. Szathmary pours flour into a plastic bag, adds salt and pepper, and tosses the smelt in it. When he has enough for a load he takes them out and starts putting them a few at a time into the hot grease in the other skillet. A call comes over the PA for a motor inspector on number two.

"I'll get that," says Jackson. "You keep on with what you're doing." When he gets back he goes to the small sink to wash his hands. "There's something I always wanted to ask you," said Sourwine. "How can you tell when your hands are dirty?"

"It's easy. Whenever I think my hands might be dirty, I wipe them on Noel's face. If they leave streaks I know I've got to wash them."

Sourwine had laid out paper plates on the card table, and as the potatoes and fish turn brown, Szathmary serves them, adding new ones to the skillet. The first plate goes to Jackson, in honor of his having spotted the smelt. Each of the five men get at least a taste of the first batch. When he finishes eating, Jackson gets up to relieve Szathmary at the stove. Many smelt are consumed.

By and by we find ourselves sitting with our feet up on the benches, picking our teeth, belching, and feeling satisfied. We begin comparing recipes, sounding like a convention of cooks. Jackson, as a southerner, is the authority on chitterlings, collard greens, butter beans, okra, and corn bread.

"Two things I can do without," I say, "chicken-fried steak and boiled peanuts. I have tasted chitterlings, although I'm not overly fond of them."

"They taste better if you don't clean the shit out before you cook them," Jackson replies.

We also discuss the relative merits of sweet potato versus pumpkin pie. Like many black people, Jackson disparages pumpkin pie, which he dismisses as a white knockoff. I respond that I don't think of pumpkin pie as white but as northern, and I like both. Sourwine has never tasted sweet potato pie.

I remind everyone about the time I made oyster stew and brought it to work. Jackson refused to eat it, then opened a jar of pickled pigs' feet.

"You won't eat oysters and you're going to eat that?"

Everyone laughs, including Jackson.

Sourwine says that all he wants every day for the rest of his life is steak for breakfast and lobster for supper.

XII

My crew and I are in the shanty for our last four-to-twelve turn, and Jackson is reminiscing about his early days in the mill.

"I was in the labor gang then, over in the rail mill, and a bunch of us laborers were sitting around, just like we are now, only there were more of us. The foreman came in and told us all to get out in the yard and start cleaning up. I was young then, and I used to spend all my days on the streets and my nights in the joints, so I counted on my time in the mill to catch up on my sleep. That night I sure didn't feel like working, so when he ordered everybody out of the shanty, instead of leaving with the rest I rolled under a bench to hide.

"I guess the foreman had the same idea I had, because after everybody else left he sat down on the bench I was under and in a few minutes I could hear him breathing like he was asleep. I didn't know what to do, so I just lay there. You can imagine what happened. I fell asleep, right there on the floor under the bench with the foreman sitting over me. You know I snore. I snored so loud I woke myself. The next thing I knew I was looking into that foreman's eyes. I guess I woke him too. Anyhow, there he was, with his head bent down under that bench, eyeballs just this far from me."

"What'd you say then?" asks Sourwine.

"What could I say? I just looked at him with a shit-eating grin and said, 'If you don't tell, I won't.' I guess he didn't, because I never heard any more about it."

Our laughter is interrupted by a call over the PA: "SOUTH END MOTOR INSPECTOR, COME TO THE HIGH-LINE. CAR DEAD."

"I'll get that one," says Jackson. He then turns to me. "You might as well come with me."

The high-line is an elevated railway that runs the length of the furnace line. It contains two sets of tracks, one for the trains that unload coke and the other for the transfer cars that run back and forth emptying iron ore and limestone to the stockhouse bins below. In addition to the main tracks there are side tracks for switching cars, and a repair area, located at the far south end of the line, with pits and cranes for working on the cars. A walkway runs parallel to the tracks.

The bed of the high-line is a grid formed by two-inch-wide rails crossing each other at right angles with a foot of space between each. Through the grid it is possible to see the stockhouse bins below into which the forty-foot-long high-line cars empty their contents. When the bins are full, the coke, iron ore and limestone comes almost up to the grid rails. When they are empty the smooth, shiny metal gates of the stockhouse bins are visible. Looking down through the grid to an empty bin gives many people a queasy stomach. The distance is enough to kill anyone who falls, even if he doesn't have a load of iron ore dropped on him.

The danger isn't actually very great. The space between the grid rails isn't wide enough to allow anyone to fall through. But someone who slips could fall on a shoulder or a wrist or land with a leg on each side of the two-inch rails, injuring the family jewels.

Even after years of trying, some people are never able to walk the highline grid. Some "walk" on all fours. There are enough workers who can do the walk, however, so that as a general rule when the maintenance foremen become aware that someone is having more than usual difficulty walking the grid, they stop assigning him there.

I did not like to walk the grid. I did discover, however, that I could fix my attention on the rails themselves and avoid looking through them to the bins below, and thus with the aid of some swearing manage to get across without slipping or throwing up.

On this particular evening as I was crossing the grid muttering god-damns and son-of-a-bitches, Jackson, walking next to me, comments, "If you think it's bad now, wait 'til when there's snow up here and you can barely make out the rails and the ice makes them twice as slippery as they are now."

We make it across the rails and climb up on the car, its lights out and air compressor idle. The car man is smoking a cigarette.

"How's things up here, peaceful?" asks Jackson.

"Oh, they been leaving us alone lately," answers the car man.

"Hickey, this is my new helper. Noel, Big Hickey. He's a big man up here."

"Pleased to meet you, sir," I say.

"Likewise, son," says Hickey. We shake hands.

Hickey stands about five-foot-eight. I wonder silently why Jackson introduced him as Big Hickey. "Did you hear about Greene getting caught with us the other night?" asks Jackson. Hickey had not, and Jackson tells him the story.

"I wonder what plans that new guy from Pittsburgh has for us up here," muses Hickey.

"I'll guess we'll find out. Well, what can we do for you?" asks Jackson.

"The car went dead on me. There was a big flash on the side about thirty yards back. I saw it out the window, and then it went dead."

"We'll fix you up good as new. We guarantee our work. If it's not working when we leave, we'll come back and work on it some more."

We leave the car and walk back on the highline to where the car man had described seeing the flash. We see that a segment of the rail that carries power to the cars is lying on the track, and a second segment is sagging dangerously.

The cars get their power from an electrified rail that runs four feet off the ground parallel to the track. The rail is made of sixteen-foot segments that are mounted on posts that are held in place by hard-rubber insulating brackets attached to the posts. Projecting from the side of the car are four-foot-long "arms" with one-foot by two-foot rocking steel plates, known as "shoes," at the end. The shoes transfer power to the car. Spring pressure on the arms keep the shoes in contact with the underside of the rail. The vibration of the car had caused a bolt holding an arm to work its way out.

76

The shoe had slipped out of position and torn two of the brackets off the posts, causing one end of the rail to fall onto the track. When the rail hit the track, the current went to ground, causing the flash and blowing the circuit breakers controlling that section of the rail. The car, now without brakes, had coasted thirty yards before stopping.

"Szathmary will need to see this," says Jackson.

We cross the grid to the highline office. From there we call over the PA for Szathmary. In a few moments the phone rings. We explain to him the trouble.

"I'll be right up."

We walk back to where the rails are torn off, and wait.

When Szathmary arrives he looks over the damage and says, "I'll start calling people out. Can you stay over?"

We look at each other and shrug. When Szathmary goes to the maintenance office, Jackson and I head to the shanty for a last cup of coffee. I take advantage of the break to ask Jackson why they call Hickey "Big."

"It's to tell him from his son, Little Hickey, in the stockhouse. It's funny, though, because Little Hickey is a lot bigger than Big Hickey. But the main reason is that he carries weight up there. Any time the foremen give the men a hard time, they can count on Big Hickey to put their case. If he thinks it is important enough, he will have them slow down or refuse overtime for a few days. That's usually enough to settle it."

"What about the union?" I ask.

"Up there, Hickey is the union. The company tried to make him a foreman, but he refused the job. They tried writing him up for little shit. That didn't work either. They noticed that when they tried that, equipment started breaking down and production fell. So they figured the smart thing was to leave him alone and let the men run things their own way."

The workers in the mill all belong to the United Steel Workers Union. But the union doesn't have much of a presence in daily life. Every few years the national organization (known as the "International" based on having members in Canada) and the company negotiate terms for wages, vacations, and job classifications; the result is a several-hundred-page contract that specifies everything to the smallest detail. The members have little choice but to ratify it when it is presented to them. Every division in the mill has an elected committeeman who processes workers' grievances. Committeemen are paid full time by the company. There are two parties, or caucuses, who compete in the elections. Each runs its slate for officers and committeemen. I attended a few union meetings shortly after I began, and found that the only people there were paid officials and those seeking to replace them. I once complained to one of the incumbents about the ineffectuality of the union.

"What's your grievance?" the official asked me.

"This job sucks."

"That's not a grievance; that's a gripe."

He meant that if the company were paying me less than the contract called for, or was assigning overtime unfairly, he could do something about it, but as for my complaint, there was nothing he could do. That about summed it up for me.

The motor inspector from the midnight shift comes in. Despite his bald head and gut, he is only twenty-nine years old, scarcely older than me.

"Sittin' on your ass drinking coffee, eh?" His accent indicated he was from somewhere in the South. "That's the way I like to see things around here. Maybe we'll get a little sleep tonight."

"Hey, Dunn, tell my helper how you got up here."

"Up yours."

"Dunn was so poor back home," explains Jackson, "that when he turned eighteen the county gave him his first pair of shoes. One of the neighbors showed him which foot to put each of them on, and when he got them on he stood up and looked down at the shoes, then he took a step backwards and looked at the shoeprint on the ground, then he took another step back and studied it some more... and walked backwards all the way from Kentucky."

Meanwhile, Szathmary is in the maintenance office calling people at home.

"Hello, this is the mill calling. Is Poulos there? Hello, Poulos, this is Szathmary. Can you come out? Good."

"Hello, this is the mill calling...."

When he has succeeded in raising eight souls from the dead, he gets back in his truck and drives back to the motor inspector shanty, where he picks up Jackson and me. We then drive to the spare parts bin. We collect and load two rail segments plus the insulators and bolts need to repair the break onto the truck. We then drive to the stairway nearest the break, get out, and carry the lighter parts up to the highline. The heavy rails would have to wait until help arrived.

It is a clear night, a bit cool—perfect for working (or sleeping). Szathmary goes back to the office to wait for the men who are coming out, and Jackson and I stay on the highline. We can see the transfer cars on the north end moving up and down the track dropping their loads through the grid. The stalled car on the south end is empty. Hickey has gone home at the end of his shift, and the midnight shift operator is catching a nap in the highline shanty.

If the rail stays down too long, the bins would run out of material and the stockhouse car operators would be unable to fill the furnaces, forcing the blowers on the south end to reduce air pressure from the stoves—"pull the wind"—an operation carried out when the quantity of raw material falls below the minimum necessary to produce iron. The main office in Pittsburgh would investigate, as they did in every case when the furnaces ceased producing iron even for a moment. That possibility, so ominous to supervisors at all levels, does not trouble in the least the sleep of the car man snoozing in the highline shanty.

The men called out from home begin showing up on the highline, grumbling about being dragged out of bed.

"I was just getting ready to sock it to Mama," says one.

"Why didn't you finish? It wouldn't have taken long," answers a second. "I heard your old lady calls you instant oatmeal, because in three minutes you're done."

"That's not what your wife says about me."

"Shee-it. If they put a muzzle on you I'd let you go by my house any time."

The last two to arrive come in Szathmary's truck. The foreman assembles the crew and makes assignments.

"Mays, you take four men and get that one rail up. Poulos, you get the other one."

I go with Poulos. It takes all five of us to carry the rail up the stairs to the highline. We throw large metal sheets over the grid to ease the crossing and eliminate the chance of someone slipping on the grid and bringing the others down with him. At a signal from Poulos, we lift the rail and carry it to the scene of the break. We lay it down and loosen the bolts that hold the old rail partly in place, allowing the rail to fall completely off. Then we lift the new rail into place.

The trick is to hold the rail steady while the brackets are put into place and the bolts inserted and tightened. The two crews cooperate to get the job done. The five men in one crew hold the rail on their shoulders while the others insert the bolts into the postholes. I feel the weight of the rail on my shoulder. Grunting and swearing, they manage to get two bolts in place, one at each end. I now feel the burden ease up. Now it is just a matter of moving the rail slightly so that the other bolts can be inserted and the whole assembly tightened into place with a large wrench.

When we are done with the first rail, we step back to allow the other crew to lift the second rail into place. This time our roles are reversed, with Mays's crew bearing the weight on their shoulders while Poulos's crew inserts the bolts in the brackets and tightens them into position. I am having difficulty locating the hole to line up the bolt.

"Put a little hair around it and you'll find it," advises Mays.

It is almost three in the morning by the time we have mounted both rails and turned the power back on so the cars can operate. When the switch is thrown, the lights on the stalled car comes on, and we all cheer.

We then start down off the highline to wash up and unwind before seeking out places to sleep. We will receive eight hours' overtime pay at time-and-a-half, and will not be expected to do any more work. Those of us who had stayed over from four to twelve get to go home at eight. Those on the day shift who had been called out at midnight will stay until four that afternoon.

I fall into place alongside Poulos. "Do they have these callouts often?"

"Whenever there's a breakdown, they call out whoever they need. Some of the guys don't come. They have their wives answer the phone and say they're not at home. One of the millwrights—I don't want to mention any names—won't even give the company his phone number, says he doesn't have a phone. They know in the office which guys won't come, so they quit asking them. As far as I'm concerned, if you work for the mill you've got an obligation to come out in an emergency. After all, this is your livelihood. If the mill shuts down, where would we be? Besides, a double looks good on payday."

We stop and stand silently, watching the big cars moving on the track carrying the ore and stone and coke that built the bridges, skyscrapers, and automobiles people take for granted. It is one of those rare moments—they often seemed to come at this time of morning—when men confide their innermost thoughts. I wonder if Poulos means what he is saying. As if reading my mind, Poulos breaks the silence.

"Kid, you got no idea how much I hate this place, how much I hate this hard hat and these steel-toed boots, how much I hate lunch meat. All these doubles I put in are for just one thing, to make sure my son won't have to spend his life out here and my daughters won't have to marry millrats."

When we get to the shanty it's full of workers. Slick is telling a story about the various mill trades.

"A customer goes into a butcher shop and sees trays of brains behind the counter: machinist brains $1.39/lb.; motor inspector brains $1.39/lb.; welder brains $1.39/lb.; and millwright brains $9.98/lb. The customer asks why millwright brains are priced so much higher than the others, and the butcher answers, 'Mister, do you know how many millwrights I got to butcher to get a pound of brains?'"

Amid the general laughter, someone asks one of the men how

he decided to become a motor inspector.

"Well, I'll tell you, it was like this. There were two jobs open, motor inspector and millwright. I didn't know what either was like, but I wanted to get out of the labor gang. I looked at the millwright and saw he was hauling around an eight-pound sledgehammer and two big pipe wrenches. His bag was so heavy he could hardly walk. Then I looked at the motor inspector and saw he had a little pouch with a couple of screwdrivers and a pair of pliers, and I knew that was what I wanted to be."

The man recounts that when he was young he spent his time chasing women. "I would have fucked a snake if they held its head. But that got old. I shifted my attention to food and became a great cook. After a while I got bored with that and took up wine. But that, too, got boring." He falls silent.

I am aware that I am being played but happy to serve as straight man. Pausing for an appropriate interval, I then ask, "What do you do now for pleasure, Joe?"

"Now I sit on the throne and have a good shit."

The conversation shifts to sleeping on the job. Sourwine says the company should provide alarm clocks so the men will know when it's time to wake up and go home.

"I know guys out here never sleep at home. They got blankets and mattresses and portable TVs," says Slick.

Jackson recalls an incident from his time on the docks. "The ore boats used to come in to unload. They had kitchens for the boat crews. The food was good, and the laborers would sneak on whenever we could. One time I went on the boat, ate a big breakfast, steak and eggs, and then I lay down. Well, I fell asleep and when I woke up I was on my way to Minnesota."

"How'd you get back?" I ask.

"I caught a return boat the next day. They didn't fire me, but I had some explaining to do at home."

Men begin to drift away to find places to sleep until shift-change, leaving me to reflect that shift work dominates not merely life in the mill but life in town. Steel workers greet each other on the street with the question, "How are you working?" While the shift work system is damaging to the workers' physical and mental health and to family life, over the years steel workers have turned it to their advantage. In one department they take turns calling in sick, allowing the men scheduled to relieve them eight hours' overtime pay. Because a couple of dozen men are involved and they rotate absences instead of reciprocating them, the pattern is not easy to spot. The result is that each worker gets an extra day off every few weeks, and then receives, a few weeks later, a paycheck with overtime, all without working a single extra hour. When the absenteeism gets too severe, the company cracks down and threatens reprisals, so the workers stop the practice for a while. Then, when the heat is off they go back to their own schedule.

In spite of our efforts to manipulate it, shift work can be a source of simmering tension among the men, which they relieve, as men do, by humor. Jackson, heading in, asks Mays, "What's your old lady cooking for breakfast? I think I'll stop by."

Mays, who is staying for the day shift, answers, "If you find a brown shoe, it's mine. I left it under your bed last night."

It was obviously not the first time the exchange has occurred. I once witnessed one man in the locker room, passing another sitting on a bench, pat the second man's bald head affectionately and say, "Your head feels as smooth as my wife's ass," to which the second man, touching his own head, said thoughtfully, "You're right, it does."

In the blast furnace division of U.S. Steel Gary Works, banter about wives, however therapeutic, never crosses the color line. Black men do not joke about having sex with white men's wives, nor the other way around. For most, this would cross a line.

Andre is renowned for the size of his penis, which won him the nickname Roto-Rooter. When one of the men complains of hemorrhoids, someone suggests that Andre could cure him without surgery. Andre admits — nay, boasts — about enjoying an occasional buggery. As he puts it, he would jump over six pussies to get to a booty. I once asked Andre if he knew the definition of homosexuality. When Andre answers no, I tell him it means having sexual relations with a person of the same sex as yourself, and it doesn't matter whether you are the active or the passive participant.

"Are you calling me a fag?"

I assure him I am not, but simply passing on what the dictionary says. Andre sees nothing shameful in buggery, so long as he was the one doing the buggering rather than the one receiving it.

Jackson and I head in, weary from our sixteen-hour shift and stiff from lying on the hard, narrow bench. On the way, we stop at the millwright shanty to pick up Sourwine and Slick. It is their last night; they will have two days off before the start of midnights.

"What do you say we stop off for breakfast?" suggests Jackson.

We meet outside the gate and go to a restaurant downtown. We all ate well, but I outdo myself, finishing off a breakfast of steak and eggs with potatoes followed by a plate of pancakes and sausage.

"Man," says Jackson. "I'd rather pay your rent than feed you."

XIII

Jackson and I meet at the maintenance office as we are putting our time cards in the rack for the first of our midnight turns. We leave the office together and start toward the shanty. The first thing we see when we step out is the side of furnace number one. The paint job is not complete and, as Greene had foretold, it shows a tremendous moon-face with a horizontal curved line suggesting a smile. Underneath, in words large enough to be read from the nearby highway, is the slogan "*Have a Safe Work Day.*"

Jackson smiles himself. "I guess the next time somebody gets hurt they'll write him up for failing to read the sign."

It is drizzling outside so we decide to go through the stockhouse. As we trudge along, stepping cautiously on the pellets scattered on the ground, we stop at each car to exchange greetings with the car man.

"Say, Taylor," calls Jackson to the number one operator. "Be careful how you sit on that car. You're liable to give it a flat tire."

Taylor is black, like all the car men, and tremendously overweight. He has been in the stockhouse for thirty years and is nearing retirement. I like him, and occasionally, on midnights, bring him a jar of coffee from the pot in the motor inspector shanty. Since the car men have no way of making their own, they are forced to rely on thermos bottles brought from home. Taylor is grateful, and shows his appreciation by explaining the operation of the car and often by diagnosing the trouble when I am unable to find it.

"Never mind," he calls back to Jackson. "I don't have nothing to do with you, anyhow." He points to me. "There's my motor inspector."

"I don't know how you did it," says Jackson as we continue northward through the stockhouse, "but you sure got Taylor on your side, and that ain't no small thing. He can be hell on the motor inspector. Before you got here, he didn't think anything of calling us down on midnights to bring him a new scale-light."

"I gave him a pack of lights and an extra rubber tool for changing them, so now he does it himself without bothering me."

"If you didn't do anything but keep Taylor happy, as far as I'm concerned, you earned your keep."

Next we see Little Hickey, the son of Big Hickey on the highline. He is taller than his father, but is a cast from the same mold: muscular, square-shouldered. He is interested in the duties of the maintenance workers, and uses some of his free time to learn about the equipment he operates. The rules decree that no employee perform duties outside of his job description. But under certain circumstances human curiosity proves stronger than the laws set up by the negotiators from management and union. Jackson tells the story of the time he had been called to fix Little Hickey's car, which wouldn't move. He couldn't locate the problem. He called Szathmary, who also was unable to find it. Szathmary declared he would go back to the officer to retrieve the drawing for the electrical controls. When he left, Jackson asked Little Hickey what was wrong with the car. "It's that relay down there," said Little Hickey, pointing to a spot on the control board. "Nobody asked me. If they treat me like a dummy I'm gonna act like a dummy." Jackson repaired it.

Once I answered a call for a skip stop and found Little Hickey waiting for me in the skiphouse, studying the control board. I showed him, as well as I was able, what the problem was and how to fix it.

Jackson and I continue on our way to the shanty. At Number Three we see Woolsey.

"How you fellows doing? I hope you're alright this evening. I hope everything is fine with you. Is everything good at home? I hope you're well, because you know I consider you two my friends, and it would hurt me if I thought you weren't well."

Woolsey utters these words in a burst of nervous speed. Everyone who sees him understands that it is wrong for him to be down in the stockhouse or in the mill at all. Now in his mid-fifties he has been off sick twice for long periods with stomach ulcers, and has returned with a nervous tic that causes him to shrug his right shoulder every ten seconds or so. Number Three furnace is the fastest on the South End, the only one with automatic stoves, requiring a larger and more constant supply of ore, coke, and limestone than the others. Woolsey normally operates his car at top speed for hours at a stretch, pausing only to call the millwrights to tighten his brakes, which come loose several times a shift because of the way he drives. He chatters in a high-pitched voice to all who pass by and converses audibly with imaginary associates. Most people avoid him, as they would a cracked boiler about to explode.

"Oh, we're fine this evening, thank you," says Jackson. "I hope you're feeling well also."

The car man on number four, Mathews, is sitting on a bench in the stockhouse. Since the men shower together they have ample opportunity to observe each other, and his exceptionally large penis is a frequent topic of conversation. In an effort to put someone at ease, he claims that it is no larger erect than when flaccid.

"He must be kidding. It's bigger soft than mine is hard," exclaims Jackson.

Jackson greets him with a big smile and a wave. "Say, Mathews, how come you ain't up there working?"

"I'm full up. The guy on four-to-twelve left me in good shape. If I put any more in it'll come out the top," he replies with a grin. "Look at the rod."

The rod is an alloy-steel bar that is lowered into the furnace through the bells. How far it falls indicates how much material is in the furnace. The result is registered in feet on a panel in the stockhouse, which the car man can read on a row of lights. The ideal level was between six and nine feet; if the material reaches any higher than six feet below the bell it will jam the furnace and prevent the bell from closing. Lower than sixteen feet is called "off the rod," indicating insufficient material, which would force the blower to "pull the wind." The rod lights on Mathews's panel show seven feet. It will be at least a half-hour before he will have to resume filling again. A good car man — and Mathews is one of the best — can pace himself to maintain a full furnace and still find time to rest.

We cross the track and go up the stairway that leads from the stockhouse to the ground level by the shanty. When we open the heavy steel door, we find the motor inspector and helper from the four-to-twelve turn awaiting our arrival impatiently.

"Where you guys been? We're waiting to go home," says Brady. It is the standard greeting of a motor inspector to his relief man, notwithstanding that Jackson and I are right on time.

Brady and his helper, Wheeler, are close. Brady is an alcoholic. It is not unusual for him to show up barely able to stand. Jackson remembers one occasion in the winter when he saw Brady striding gaily down the road with his light coat thrown over his shoulder, smiling broadly and singing about a car with no wheels. The only thing that kept him from freezing to death was the anti-freeze he had swallowed earlier. On the evenings he showed up drunk he would hit the bench and sleep soundly for two hours. During that time Wheeler would answer all the calls. Wheeler never complained about the arrangement, and never said a word about Brady's drinking. He simply anticipated his drinking bouts — the night after payday was a certainty — and made sure he himself was in good shape.

"Go on home, Brady," says Jackson, winking at Wheeler. "Everything OK around here?"

"Top shape."

Jackson and I are sitting in the shanty drinking coffee when Slick walks in. He has just returned from the stockhouse where he had been adjusting the brakes on a car.

"I was talking with some of the brothers in the labor gang," he begins in his gravelly voice. "I asked them why they don't do somethin' with their lives instead of smokin' dope all the time? You know what they told me? 'Whitey ain't no good.' Here I am, fifty-three years old, and they're telling me Whitey ain't no good."

I feel honored that Slick tells this story in my presence. It isn't the first time we have talked about race, and it is obvious that I have won Slick's confidence.

XIV

Of the three thousand or so "acceptable men" in the blast furnace division of U.S. Steel's largest mill, maybe a couple of dozen were female. They are classified as laborers, the lowest pay grade in the mill. Some of them are girlfriends of supervisors; they are mostly white and work in the offices, answering phones and carrying messages from one department to another. Black women and some white women worked around the blast furnaces. But none of the women had to work very hard. I once asked a black woman with whom I had become friendly and who spent her days pushing piles of dirt back and forth, if her husband knew how easy she had it. She laughed and said, "No, he thinks I kill myself out here, and I want to keep it that way."

The women's work around the blast furnaces, although easy, is dirty, and is not generally regarded as "women's work." The female laborers for the most part laugh at these conventions, reminding their family and friends that they make more money than many of those who hold traditional "female jobs" in offices. They wage an unceasing battle to keep their hair and bodies clean. They have their own washroom, where they shower and change clothes. Men are supposed to be barred from the women's washroom. However, one of the men, who presents with what he thinks are "feminine mannerisms," thought his special qualities made it OK for him to walk freely through the women's washroom. The women complained bitterly about it, and called him names when he came through, but nothing was ever done.

One of the women at the mill was an American Indian from northern Minnesota. She told me that when she was younger she and the other Indian kids used to gather wild rice and sell it to the health food store. She had six kids and an abusive white husband who had done time for burglary, where he learned the art of buggery, which he practiced on her. She wore a blonde wig. The black women didn't like her because they thought she was trying to pass for white. She had a thing for me, but I wasn't interested.

One of the black women had worked at a factory that made machine tools; she bid on a crane operator's job and got a tryout. The white men in the department refused to break her in. Contrary to their usual practice, whenever she was on the crane they would hook up the loads off balance, and in general did what they could to make her job harder than necessary. After a few weeks she called them together at the time clock and delivered a speech: "Listen, you motherfuckers, I see you all waiting here every day to see if I'm coming in or not. Well, it won't work. I'm not leaving. I'm not asking for special consideration as a woman. I just want to be respected as a crane operator. I've got rent to pay and babies to feed just like you, so I don't care what you do, you're not running me out of here." According to her, they changed their attitudes after that and became totally cooperative.

Dorothy is one of the black women in the labor gang. Aware that she had grown up in the city and knew many people, I asked her about a factory nearby that made railway cars and was famous for its frequent unauthorized, or "wildcat," strikes. I also ask her why similar things don't happen at the mill. Her answer:

"It's because the people here are always on strike."

I was impressed with her insight. Once she led me to the little "store" in a nook where a few black workers sold gloves and canned goods and introduced me to them. I unthinkingly put a foot up on an empty bench and was rewarded with a dirty look from their chief. Self-conscious, I took my foot down. After they left, she reprimanded me. It stung, but I knew she was right. She disappeared from the mill for several months. I was wondering what had become of her, and asked one of the other women. The woman was reluctant to answer. "I get it," I said, "female trouble." The woman said nothing.

Management decided to reassign the women from the labor gang to work on the furnace floor. The position represented a big pay hike for the labor gang, but it was also hotter, dirtier, and more dangerous. Most of the women didn't like the change, but thought there wasn't much they could do about it. Before they did it, they reassigned the white women who were working around the blast furnaces to work in the offices, answering phones, carrying messages etc., so that only the black women were sent to the furnace floor. One of the white women, Mary, a southerner, refused the reassignment. She said, "I'm staying with my friends." As a result, she was sent to the furnace floor. The black women loved her, called her "Proud Mary."

When the company assigned the black women in the labor gang to work on the furnace floor, I thought it presented an opportunity. I approach several black workers in the maintenance gang to see what they thought; each of them tell me, "See Floyd."

Floyd is one of the more experienced in the millwright gang. I stop him one day and ask if we can talk. Floyd agreed, and we set a time. When we meet, I lay out my view as forcefully as I can: "They've gone too far this time. Can we let them get away with this?"

Floyd listens without committing himself. His non-reaction reminds me that Floyd has no reason to trust me. I am white and have only been in the mill for a short time. He knew that Jackson and Slick think I'm OK, and I knew enough of the black grapevine to think they had spoken about me to Floyd, but apparently it wasn't enough.

A few months earlier, Jackson told me about Randall, a black foreman who had been a millwright and now found himself in charge of a mostly-white maintenance crew on the night shift. Night shift foremen, whatever their background, are expected to be familiar at least with the rudiments of both the electrical and mechanical aspects of the work. Randall was up to speed on the mechanical side but lacked electrical experience. He suspected that some of the white electrical workers under him were taking advantage of his ignorance to get over on him. Jackson and Randall were friendly, and Randall had asked Jackson if he could help. Jackson in turn told me and asked if I had any books on electrical work that could help Randall.

I understood that their shared experience as victims of color prejudice in the mill had created a bond between Jackson and Randall. But I was initially surprised that Jackson was asking me to cross the line between worker and supervisor, a line which in my experience in other industries was rarely crossed. Without hesitation I answered yes, thinking that in this case the need for solidarity with a black foreman overrode any feelings I might have for the white electricians under Randall's charge. I was aware that I would be considered to be a race traitor by some of the whites. But I passed on what I had to Jackson, who, I assumed, passed them on to Randall. I was pleased that Jackson had enough confidence in me to ask for my help.

A few months later, I find myself working under Randall, something which rarely happens because we normally work different shifts. That night we are changing cars in the stockhouse. As it happened, I'm wearing regular street shoes in place of the Frankenstein shoes with the steel toes and metatarsal guards that are regulation. I jump onto one of the cars, and Randall, glancing at my shoes, raises his eyebrows. But doesn't write me up for a safety violation as he could have done. I reflect on how much information had been conveyed in that glance. Later on, I ask Jackson if he had told Randall where the books he was using had come from. Jackson said he had.

My brief exchange with Floyd taught me how group dynamics work among black workers. According to the ideal of American society, any of the several workers I approached with my idea of doing something about the company's latest outrage toward the black women might have promised to talk to others, or, even invite me to a meeting where I could present my ideas. Instead, they all, without exception, advised me to "See Floyd."

What was going on? After considerable reflection, I conclude that for the black workers in the maintenance department of the blast furnace division of the largest plant of the largest steel-manufacturing company in the world, some things are more important than formal democracy—in a word, cohesion. Their experience has taught them it is more important to stand together than for each to have his day. Floyd had earned their respect, and so long as he held it they would defer to him. If he lost it, or moved away, or died, they would replace him. I think that lesson is probably transferrable to the world beyond. It squares with what a friend of mine, a black man who had been a gangbanger before he became a political activist, had told me.

"Whenever I meet with a new group of people I always look for the one guy who the others look to. He may not be the one who does the talking, but he will be the one people's eyes turn toward."

My friend was thinking mainly of black people, but I think his observation applies to others.

When it appeared that nothing had come of my conversation with Floyd, I decide to act on my own. I make up a leaflet. To make it seem more authentic than the printed leaflets distributed at the gates by one or another radical group, I write it out by hand, make fifty copies at the public library, and smuggle them into the mill, leaving them where I thought they would be seen. The following week another leaflet appears, typed and printed. Management goes ahead with the changes. The protest I hoped for did not occur.

ATTENTION (1973)

THE COMPANY HAS REACHED A NEW LOW FOR DIRTY TRICKS. THEY ARE SENDING THE WOMEN UP ON THE FURNACES TO WORK CLAYMAN.

TO MAKE THINGS WORSE THEY HAVE ASSIGNED THE WHITE WOMEN TO OFFICE JOBS SO THAT ONLY THE BLACK SISTERS WILL BE SENT ON THE FURNACES.

THEY MUST NOT BE PERMITTED TO GET AWAY WITH THIS. THE WOMEN ARE FIGHTING, BUT THEY NEED HELP. (AS USUAL, NO HELP CAN BE EXPECTED FROM THE UNION.)

DISCUSS WITH FRIENDS NEAR YOU WHAT ACTION TO TAKE TO PREVENT THIS OUTRAGEOUS INJUSTICE. IF WE DON'T STOP THIS INDECENCY, WE HAVE NO RIGHT TO HOLD OUR HEADS UP

(PASS THIS ALONG)

SLAVE TRIBUNE

Over the past two (2) months more women have been hired in at Gary Works. 98% are Afro- American, like most Afro-American they are hired into the Blast - Furnace, Sintering Plants, Coke Plant, Open Hearts and Ore Docks, which are the lowest paid, dirtest, hottest and most degrading jobs.

We all know that this is racism. But what has happened in the last two months is another chapter added to the history of Gary Works racist policy.

Afro-American women have been placed in the Blast Furnace Stock House and Blast Furnaces as clay women. In the Stock House the women does pit work, which is a strain on men, they use 15 inch scoops to lift heavy materials over their heads. On the Blast Furnaces the clay women are forced to dig clay, push wheelbarrows of clay and sand up hill, lift heavy gates and bare the intense heat. On the Ore Docks sisters are forced into boats to shovel ore and are made to lift pens and lids from the boats.

It should be noted that these women are forced into the pits, boats and on the furnaces by racist slave drivers and puppet supervisors. Are these people sane? NO! An act of racism is an act of insanity and ignorance. These racist people are perpetuator of discrimination. dehumanlization and exploitation etc. (modern words for slavery). Moreover, the racist supervisors are trying to make sure that Afro-American does not escape from their inferiorty complex.

Some of the women are complining of backaches, soreness and of being unable to do their home chores after returning to their families from work.

Johannesburg South Africa is a long way from Gary works, but there is a compareson between the two. In South Africa black male slaves are forced int the deep and dangerous mines with no saftey to protect the workers while the black african sisters are forced to use sluge-hammer, picks shovels and axs, to pick, dig, bust huge stones and carry railroad crosstires to build railroads to the mines. In the mean time Afro-American males are forced to work in the dirtiest, hottest, lowest paid and most degrading jobs, the Afro-American sisters are forced to pick up the spillage from these dirtest, hottest lowest paid and most degrading jobs.

These racist, insane and inhuman treatment of the sisters must be brought to an end for once and for all.

Workers must unite to stop these acts.

PROTECT OUR WOMEN

UNITY IS THE WORKERS WEAPON

XV

The duties of the cast house crew: The frontside crew have to clean up after every cast. Scrap and slag must be removed and the runners made good with sand, clay, etc.... The disposal points for scrap and rubbish should be easily reached.... Control rooms and workmen's shelters must be provided with two means of exit. All water discharges should be clearly visible from floor level. It should be possible to wheel a loaded barrow to any part of the cast house and completely round the furnace. A hurried departure from around the taphole is undesirable. Good lighting and ventilation are essential. Furnace crews have to remain in the immediate vicinity and must eat when the job permits.... A cast house is never a drawing room, nor an easy place to work.

"MOTOR INSPECTOR COME TO NUMBER THREE FURNACE. CAN'T GET THE MUDGUN IN THE HOLE." Brady and Wheeler, the motor inspectors on duty, can't get the mud gun to operate. Iron overflows the trenches. Three men are killed. The company releases a statement saying that they were taken to the local hospital where they were pronounced dead. The local newspaper carries the U.S. Steel's statement.

Everyone knows it's bunk. The men were dead as soon as the flowing iron hit their bodies. I write a statement correcting the company's account. Several men from the blast furnace division sign it. We send it off to the newspaper, which prints it with the names of the signers.

XVI

Andre is a motor inspector. His job is to do electrical repairs on mill equipment. The wiremen, another electrical trade, are more highly rated than the motor inspectors, because they are not limited to maintaining existing equipment but are responsible for installing new equipment. They are more highly paid than the motor inspectors, and also work straight day turns Monday through Friday. The biggest difference between the two is that the wiremen are eligible to take the test for licensed electricians, which means they could escape the mill and work "in town." The wiremen look down on the motor inspectors, who resent them for it. The tension is exacerbated by the color line. The wiremen in the blast furnace division are all white, while the motor inspectors include both white and black. After ten years as a motor inspector, Andre decides he wants to become a wireman, and bids on an opening. The company stalls, does everything they can to discourage him. They are finally compelled to let him in — but they decide that he would have to drop ten pay grades and start over as an apprentice, even though as a motor inspector he has already gained a basic knowledge of electricity. Eager to qualify for an electrician's license and escape from the mill, Andre agrees. Thus the lily-white wireman's trade is breached.

Black workers first entered Gary Works during the First World War, when the increased demand for labor combined with the drying up of European immigration forced the industry to open its doors to them. They made up between 10 and 15 percent of the workforce, and were rigidly confined to the lowest categories of unskilled labor. In 1919, three hundred sixty-five thousand steelworkers struck nationwide. The strike was defeated after three months.

In the course of the strike twenty-two were killed, hundreds beaten and shot, and thousands arrested. It was conducted under the auspices of twenty-four craft unions, all of which excluded black workers. Not surprisingly, black workers refused to support the strike, and it was widely acknowledged that they "broke the great steel strike."

The United Steel Workers of America, organized on industrial rather than craft lines, came into the mill following the sit-down strikes in the automobile industry in 1936–37. According to the story, U.S. Steel's CEO wished to avoid a repetition of the experience in the auto industry. In that case workers occupied the General Motors plant in Flint, Michigan, for forty-four days, defying the threats of company thugs, police, and National Guard to evict them. He also wished to avoid the experience of a mill in Colorado where the workers had walked off the job decades earlier leaving a solid block of iron in the furnace. So he struck a deal with the head of the union federation which was seeking to organize the steel industry.

While the new union accepted black members, it continued the tradition of confining them to the worst jobs. The first contract between it and the company established the principle of division seniority, which meant that any seniority workers accumulated applied only within their division—coke plant, blast furnace, open hearth, rolling mills, etc.. Moreover it established within each division separate tracks for production and maintenance workers. Many black workers who had come to the mill during World War II and Korea had accumulated seniority, which they might have expected would allow them to move up. But they found themselves locked in to where they started. U.S. Steel Gary Works ran seven miles long and two miles deep along the southern shore of Lake Michigan. Moving from east to west, the divisions ran from crude (the coke plant) to finish (the rolling mills), from dirty to comparatively clean, and from black to white. Pay scales ranged widely within each division. For some years there had been grumblings among black workers about racial discrimination, and some had filed lawsuits.

When Dorothy returns to the mill, we resume our conversations. She tries to recruit me as an agent for a soap and cosmetics company that operates on a pyramid scheme. Those who invest the most money are known as "generals" and are granted the right to sell their products in a territory, and, more importantly, the right to employ sub-agents, known as "captains," for a share of their commission on sales. The sub-agents in their turn employ sub-sub-agents, known as "lieutenants." Dorothy is a "lieutenant." The real money is made not from selling soap and cosmetics but from selling the sub-rights; Dorothy's apartment was full of unsold soap and cosmetics. The "officers" attend annual conventions at which the company's founder and CEO, a hillbilly in a polyester suit, delivers inspirational talks that appeal to people's desire for something more than the ordinary. Although I had no interest in the scheme, I recognized that its appeal to her rested on more than monetary ambition. For her it represents a search for community, and I respond sympathetically.

Dorothy tells me her absence was due to what used to be called a nervous breakdown.

"I've been in prison, I've been in a mental hospital, and I've worked in the mill, and as far as I'm concerned this place is the weirdest of all. At least in those other places people knew something was wrong; around here people think what they do is normal."

I believe that anyone who isn't a bit crazy in this society is lacking in sensitivity, or character, or something, so I am not put off by this. She believes that the bond between her, a black woman, and me, a white man, represents the key to overturning existing social relations, since in her view black men and white women are generally too trapped in social conventions to ever break out.

At one point, Dorothy and I drive together to Mississippi to visit a friend of mine. I had never been to the South and did not know what to expect. I worried about the reaction to a white man and black woman traveling together. Every place we go we are greeted warmly and sent off with the standard parting, "Y'all come back now, heah?" I wonder how we would have been greeted had the sexes been reversed. In Tennessee I taste fried catfish and hushpuppies for the first time; I loved them. The one exception was Southern Illinois, where a cafe refused to serve us. We ordered ice cream and were told the restaurant was "out." I remembered that the area had been historically defined by excluding black people from the coal mines.

Dorothy wants me to move in with her, but she is allergic to my dog; we maintain separate residences.

"I've lost out to other women. I even lost out to a car. This is the first time I finished second to a dog."

The two of us agree to call a meeting to address discrimination in the mill. The meeting is at my home, the brick two-bedroom bungalow on the East Side. A few friends show up. I am the only non-black person among the half-dozen or so present.

The first issue that comes up is should our effort address both race and sex discrimination or confine itself to race. The black men present all feel that it should confine itself to race, that to raise the issue of sex discrimination would be to subject the movement to ridicule. Dorothy argues that it should address both. I am mostly quiet through the debate. Then I speak on her side, saying that it is necessary to reach out to all those who might side with us. My intervention sways the others, and the group agrees to pursue both complaints. I believe the resolution has meaning. Had the group not been willing to take up the issue of sex discrimination I would still have supported the effort. Whereas if a women's group refused to address race discrimination, I would have had seen it as the enemy and had nothing further to do with it.

We plan another meeting. Because we expect it to be larger, and with the union hall closed to us, we hold it in a church that had hosted other gatherings. Twenty people show up, including Jackson and Lorenzo Parmer, the blast furnace committeeman who ruled the division like a ward leader in Chicago. Parmer's presence indicates the union officials are scared. Once again, I am the only non-black person present.

Dorothy opens the meeting. She says the plan is to file a lawsuit, and appeals for people to sign onto it. Parmer speaks at length, saying that it would be a mistake to go up against the union, which, in spite of shortcomings, was "our friend." One of his assistants follows with the same message. I sit fuming in silence.

Jackson speaks next.

"We've been doing it your way for a long time, and it hasn't worked. Why don't we give these people a chance?"

Several people nod in agreement, and at the end come up and ask to be included. Afterwards, Jackson tells me:

"I could see you were mad, and I understood why you didn't say anything. I figured I had to speak up."

I was deeply appreciative.

Meanwhile, Billy Harkins, a young black man from Covington, Tennessee, who has worked in the mill for six years as a laborer and stockhouse car operator, decides to challenge Parmer for the position of blast furnace committeeman. He was pursuing a junior college degree in labor studies and sociology, and is part of the group led by Little Hickey. He has worked with civil rights organizations in Tennessee and in the mill town. Billy puts out a printed flyer. It is the first time anyone could remember that Parmer has faced opposition, and certainly the first time he has faced the printed word. The flyer read in part:

"One of the most flagrant forms of discrimination against minority groups has been the system of divisional seniority, whereby black workers are assigned to certain units, such as iron producing, and 'locked in' low paying jobs, unable to transfer to better jobs in other areas of the mill. I pledge, whether or not I am elected, to fight so that black, Latin, and white workers in the iron producing division will have the right to bid on jobs in other areas of the plant, based on mill seniority. I will fight for full and honest posting of all jobs within the division, and for tests directly related to the job in question."

In addition, Billy pledged:

"If I am elected, the practice of the griever talking to supervision before discussing the problem with the concerned worker will end. I will take steps to end the 'special agreements' that have been made in this division, such as forcing employees to 'make up' lost time instead of paying them for valid claims. I would like to see at least one woman assistant griever, to represent the special needs of female employees. I will regularly provide information, in the mill, about current problems. And I intend to encourage every work gang to organize and directly involve itself in settling disputes that arise with the company."

I face a dilemma. I am skeptical of campaigns within the union, regarding them mostly as a distraction from the struggle. If people are going to engage with existing structures, better the courts, which might reflect public opinion, than an entrenched bureaucracy. On the other hand, I like Billy and want to help my friend. I know him and his family well. We visit each other and talk often, and *The Calumet Insurgent Worker* published a memoir Billy wrote of his civil rights work in the South. So I kept my reservations to myself and did what I could to help.

Jackson served as Billy's campaign manager. Billy was elected.

It is a period of hope for labor union reformers. I attend a meeting at the public library at where people from several mills in the region, encouraged by the recent success of a reform caucus in the coal miner's union, promote the idea of launching a similar effort in steel. I point out that the victory of the reformers in the coal miners' union was illusory, that the new leadership turned out to be no different from the bunch they ousted. I find neither echo nor answer.

The reformers decide to mount a challenge to the incumbent regime in the union. They choose as their candidate a man who had been president of a big union local nearby and who was now district director — elected by a big margin after an initial election was overturned in court on the grounds that the incumbent had committed fraud (including that the union leadership at our mill had faked ballots). His backers called themselves "Progressive Steelworkers of America." Opponents charged them with being "communist."

I have always been skeptical of union reform. In my view the union, at best, is a defensive organization, but something more is needed to free the working class from its subordination to capital. I supported Billy in his campaign for blast furnace committeeman on the grounds of friendship, but there is no way I am getting involved in union reform nationwide.

While I am reflecting on what course to follow, the U.S. Labor Department charged one of the other steel companies with failure to act against racial discrimination and ordered it to make sweeping changes in the seniority system.

STO distributes an issue of *The Calumet Insurgent Worker* with the lead article on the Labor Department's order. We call it a response to wildcat strikes and walkouts over the past few years. We also report the statements of Gary Works officials denying its relevance to them. And we print the statement of a local white union official calling the order "reverse discrimination." *The Calumet Insurgent Worker* comments that evidently he prefers the upfront discrimination that has existed all along. "He shares the feeling of many white workers at the plant that an equal chance for black workers means discrimination against the whites."

"Interviews show that many white workers believe that blacks were being 'pushed ahead' of them while black workers were fully aware of the increase in friction that would result from the ruling."

The Calumet Insurgent Worker runs letters from black workers at three local steel plants recounting the discrimination they face. In their willingness to challenge both company and union, our (STO) little band of fewer than a dozen people stands alone against the various other radical groups that infest the mill but fail to champion the black workers' complaints.

The federal agency responsible for enforcing civil rights legislation files a suit against the nation's nine largest steel producers, including U.S. Steel, for discriminatory hiring, promotion, assignment, and wage policies directed against women and minorities. The suit names the United Steelworkers of America as a co-defendant.

After five-and-a-half months of secret negotiations, the government and the defendants work out a consent decree overturning division seniority and providing that seniority would now be determined on the basis of plant service. The companies and the union also agree to a set of goals which include hiring women and minority persons for half the openings in trade and craft jobs and for

25 percent of the vacancies in supervisory jobs. The decree also provides for approximately $31 million in back pay to be distributed to about 40,000 minority and women employees. It comes to about $700 for every employee, pro-rated for years of service — for a century of discrimination.

The checks, when they come, range from $300 to $990. Right above the line workers have to sign to cash the check is a statement waiving the recipient's right to sue for further damages. To endorse the check was to sign the waiver.

In the issue that reported on the Labor Department action, *The Calumet Insurgent Worker* runs a statement in large letters: "The publishers of this newsletter are willing to lend whatever energy and resources we have to a campaign against racial discrimination in hiring and promotion." One of STO's members, Kingsley Clarke, is an attorney. He makes himself available to hear complaints without charge.

Black steelworkers come to see him, enraged by the paltry amount of their checks. They want to sue. They are not going to waive their right to go to federal court. One worker says, "I thought I would at least get a mule," and threw his check in the wastebasket. "No way I am going to sign that."

The attorney replies, "Yes, indeed, that is what I am here for. We can go to federal court. You absolutely deserve more than the paltry $574. I do, however, want you to know a couple of things. The steel companies and USWA will immediately hit us with discovery requests, depositions that will cost us about $1,000 even if only taped. When we go to federal court you and I will be sitting at a table on one side of the courtroom. Arrayed against us will be lawyers for the government, the companies, and the USWA, the fanciest money can buy."

I am thinking of the scene from "The Fortune Cookie," where the ambulance-chasing lawyer "Whiplash Willie Gingrich" (Walter Matthau) is filing a personal injury suit against the National Football League on behalf of his brother-in-law (Jack Lemmon). He walks into the office of the lawyers for the NFL with their two-thousand-dollar suits, floor-to-ceiling shelves of leather-bound law books and four-inch thick rug.

The worker who had just tossed his check in the waste basket looks at the attorney's scraggly beard and torn blue jeans and then turns around looking at the church basement where we are meeting.

"This sucks," he says "but my wife says that $574 would make two car payments." He fishes the check out of the wastebasket and endorses it.

XVII

I complete my apprenticeship and start classes. I'm assigned to work on the North End, without a helper. One of the furnaces is acting up, and I have to babysit it, which means throwing a switch every hour or so, a switch that should have been operating automatically. I welcome the assignment, as it gives me the opportunity to stay warm and catch some sleep between throws.

However, as often happens in the mill, I get an emergency call from the foreman on another furnace. My presence is required immediately.

"I'm supposed to stay here and watch number nine," I tell the foreman.

"Never mind that," he says. "I'm telling you I need you here."

"Very well," I say, and in compliance with the well-known rule that the last order received was the one obeyed, I leave my comfortable perch on the bench in number nine skip house to answer the foreman's call. I leave only after making sure that the switch I was supposed to throw every hour would soon kick out, causing the furnace to cease operating, and also making sure that my new assignment is out of range of the PA system.

Things take their course. I am away for an hour, the switch fails, and they had to "pull the wind" on number nine. The next morning when I pass through the maintenance office, Marlowe asks me what had happened. I explain that I had been called away and was unable to hear the PA. My explanation is deemed satisfactory. It is determined that thereafter no one would work alone on the North End. And I achieve renown as the one who had saved the helpers' jobs on the North End. It is a source of pride for me, along with "Noel's sticky tape."

A popular film set in the Calumet Region depicts a scene in which a company representative shows up at a high-school class and gives a talk to the students about the careers that await them in the steel industry. One of the students stands up and declares they will not spend their lives the way their parents did. The students join her in singing "Hit the Road, Jack," and run him out. I regret it was only a film.

It is management's custom to hire local college students to work summers when they are on break from school, to bolster their standing in the community and with the hope that some of those they hire might later work for U.S. Steel in one capacity or another. One of those hired was Jackson's son, Darryl, who is attending a local community college. Ordinarily they assign the students to work as laborers, pushing piles of dirt from here to there and back again. Someone in the office with a sense of humor assigns Darryl to work as my helper. We knew each other well from the times Jackson and I had spent together. I tell Darryl what his father had said about keeping his kids out of the mill when we first met. We laugh about it.

Construction is proceeding on the new furnace, touted as being the "most modern in the western hemisphere" (meaning outside of Japan). To prepare, the blast furnace division organizes classes for maintenance workers who would be working there. I am included. When Marlowe tells me of the assignment, he warns he doesn't want me "stirring up the troops." I took it as a reference to the letter in the local daily. It was the only response I heard from anyone in authority.

The classes are scheduled once a week for four hours starting at 8 a.m. After a midnight shift I find it impossible to stay awake in class, listening to someone drone on about circuitry. I nod off repeatedly, snoring audibly, to my embarrassment and the amusement of my fellow students. They draw paper "open eyes" for me to put under my glasses. After a few weeks they drop me from the classes. It doesn't seem to matter. When they open the new furnace they assigned me there anyhow.

On the "most modern furnace in the western hemisphere,"

nothing works as it is supposed to. Dozens of laborers are assigned to tasks that are supposed to be done by automated equipment. Supervisors seek to conceal the reality from the higher-ups. When big shots from U.S. Steel headquarters in Pittsburgh tour the mill, the laborers are ordered to hide. One of the big shots opens a closed door and finds a couple of dozen laborers in various positions of repose. The incident reminds me of the rumor that the person who takes home the most money in each division is the one who compiles the records of the division's output. Since everyone's bonuses from workers to division superintendents depend on output, they all bribe him to inflate the figures. Consequently, management has no real idea of how much steel is being produced. Whether the rumor is true, I cannot say.

Billy's election as committeeman for the blast furnace division does not meet expectations. Wages are unchanged since they are set by the national contract, but conditions get worse. Billy had pledged to end the "special relationship" between the union and management, represented by the practice of "swapping grievances" rather than taking disputes through the established procedure. When he tries to carry out his campaign promise, the division management, with the approval of the higher authorities, strike back.

The first arrangement to fall is the little store that Dorothy's friends had set up where they sold canned goods and other supplies workers needed. The division superintendent orders them to shut it down. Next, the supervisors increase the number of their surprise visits to the maintenance shanties and wash house to catch and write up people for rule violations. They begin enforcing arbitrary and pointless rules they had previously overlooked, such as requiring safety glasses or hard hats in situations where they were unnecessary. Wherever the maintenance trades had divided the work among themselves in ways that made sense but ignored the boundaries between them, supervisors write people up for crossing job lines.

These changes, instead of producing a mood of rebellion, as might have been predicted, have the opposite effect. People begin to grumble at the disappearance of the petty privileges that made life tolerable. How can dignity outweigh an early lunch from time to time? Discontent spreads, and people who had voted for Billy begin to regret having ousted the *ancien regime*.

Dorothy is driven to despair by the mood of surrender among people she had grown up, gone to school, and worked with, and for whom she had, for a moment, entertained hopes. She has another breakdown. My relationship with her does not survive.

Without either personal ties or a job, no one would choose to live near the mill in Gary. The little group of former students I had recruited, who had dedicated themselves for a few years to political work in the mill town, resume their previous career paths, deciding that social work and the caring professions make for more comfortable lives than emptying bed pans in the county hospital.

In Russia, unsuccessful revolutionaries of an earlier generation were sent to Siberia; in Germany they were battered to death in the back of automobiles and their lifeless bodies thrown into the Landswehr Canal; in China they fell before Chiang Kai-shek's firing squads; in my generation in Indonesia they were slaughtered and thrown into rivers in such numbers that for months people refused to eat fish; in Chile they were dispatched from soccer fields. In the U.S. black revolutionaries I knew personally went to prison for decades or were murdered in their beds, while so-called whites went to... graduate school.

One of my comrades in STO, after years in factories, returned to the university he attended as an undergraduate, to get a degree in education. He urges me to join him.

"Spend a year in the library. See how you like it."

I take him up on the suggestion. Harvard University prided itself on admitting one or two students from "non-traditional" backgrounds to the master's of education program every year. (The other one this year is an Aboriginal woman from Australia who, like me, lacked a BA. Which of us is more out of place?) I did well enough that the university made me an offer I couldn't refuse. So it came to pass that some years after riding in the 1940s-era bus through a gate under a massive arch with the name of U.S. Steel's founder etched on it onto the grounds of the largest works of the largest steel company in the U.S., I find myself sitting in a leather armchair looking out through two-story windows onto the Charles River in Cambridge, Massachusetts. There are Oriental rugs on the floor and bound volumes of *Punch* on the shelves. As I am listening to gifted undergraduates play a Schubert quintet, I think that if the rest of the fellas back in Gary found out how good I had it, they would all leave and there would be nobody left to make steel.

I manage for a few years to stay in touch with Jackson, who tells me, "They can't make us old guys work, but they sure are whipping the asses of the young people."

On the two-hundredth anniversary of the Republic, Gary Works management decided to clean up some areas, build walkways, and throw open the gates of U.S. Steel Gary Works, the largest works of the largest steel mill in the world to public tours. People from all over the world come to wonder at the "Industry that made America Great."

Advance Praise for *Acceptable Men*

Acceptable Men tells a tale neither of regret nor escape. Noel Ignatiev's experiences at U.S. Steel Gary Works are offered as a key to his academic and political commitments. On full display is Noel's skill at letting the details of the daily lives and struggles of working people illuminate broader trends and teach valuable lessons. *Acceptable Men* is a segment of a larger work left unfinished. We should not dwell on that loss. Our task as readers is to carry Noel's spirit and insights into the struggles of our day.

— **John H. Bracey**, Professor in the W.E.B. Du Bois Department of Afro-American Studies at the University of Massachusetts, Amherst

In his years in the steel mill, Noel was a student—a student of the organization of production, of the profound skills that workers acquired, of workers' deep-seated convictions and sometimes quite fantastic notions of why things are the way they are, of the foolishness of the supervisors, of the shallowness of corporate propaganda, and of the unexpected friendships that developed across the fault lines of job hierarchies, race and gender. Noel probably knew how to tell a good story before his time in the mill, but his time there allowed him to perfect his talent. It is on rich display in this memoir.

— **John Garvey** is on the editorial board of *Hard Crackers* as well as *Insurgent Notes*.

Noel Ignatiev's thick description of his life working at Gary, Indiana's U.S. Steel plant is one for the ages. His combining of the technical details of steel making, irreverent comradery, accounts of racism both in the plant and in the country as a whole, with damning matter-of-fact indictments of the company's total lack of concern for the safety of its workers, makes this a must read for all who want deeper insights into U.S. society and capitalism in general.

— **Michael Goldfield**, author of *The Southern Key: Class, Race, and Radicalism in the 1930s and 1940s*

This book is laugh-out-loud funny and packed with conversations that appear verbatim, from a steel mill in the early 1970s. It is a snapshot of the gone world of industrial production, with precise descriptions of the blast furnace, and a step-by-step accounting of interactions among workers and between workers and bosses. It is a brilliant exposition of the daily workings of race and power with hardly a word of interpretation, that moves along like a novel while revealing the disparities between what people do and what they think they think, and showing how workers cooperate in the struggle to take back their time and dignity, prefiguring a new society. The bulk of it was written in 1973.

I showed it to a friend who worked at Great Lakes Steel on Zug Island and he told me, "Noel worked in the absolute worst part of the mill. The blast furnaces, cinder plant and coke ovens are like hell on Earth.... I absolutely loved his depictions of his co-workers. I laughed and laughed. He really nailed them."

This is the primary material that informed the *Race Traitor* project and *How the Irish Became White* and it is an enduring portrait of proletarian life in elegant, accessible language.

— **Beth Henson** was a member of the Sojourner Truth Organization and is author of *Agrarian Revolt in the Sierra of Chihuahua, 1959–1965* (Tucson: University of Arizona Press, 2019).

In his posthumous memoir, in the manner of Dante Aligheri or Maxim Gorky, Noel Ignatiev takes us on a tour of the "lower depths" of U.S. Steel's Gary Works. Ignatiev shows us the various ploys with which steel workers attempted to take back some of the socially necessary labor power that US Steel had stolen from them. Some ploys were humorous. All were tragic — even when they netted workers a temporary respite in the form of a little sleep on a hard bench in a changing room or a raucous card game while still on the clock. For black workers, especially those who were skilled or semi-skilled, many such efforts were shaded by white supremacy — which made them doubly tragic. In an age where a significant portion of the national workforce has been warehoused because of capital flight, technological innovation and now a pandemic virus, Ignatiev's memoir is a must-read.

> —**John E. Higginson**, Professor Emeritus of History, University of Massachusetts, Amherst, and the author of *A Working Class in the Making: Belgian Colonial Labor Policy, Private Enterprise and the African Mine Worker, 1907–1951* and *Collective Violence and the Agrarian Origins of South African Apartheid 1900–1948*.

Our comrade Noel Ignatiev died in 2019. He left with us this remarkable 110-page memoir. In it he describes his experience after being hired at the U.S. Steel Gary Works, "the largest works of the largest steel company in the world." At first glance the story is one of hilarious work evasion by fellow workers. In contrast to work on an assembly line, Noel and his family at work spent much of their time playing cards, shooting the breeze over coffee, and catching up on sleep. Two underlying facts pierce this surface impression. The first is the almost total irrelevance of the local union of the United Steelworkers of America to which all hourly employees belonged. As Noel explains, "I have always been skeptical of union reform. In my view the union, at best, is a defensive organization, but something more is needed to free the working class from its subordination to capital."

The second fact is the overwhelming importance of contesting the employer's racial discrimination as the necessary first step in nurturing "our vision of mass organization independent of the unions." Indeed, Noel's growing relationship with a particular black worker, Jackson, is the glue which holds together the entire fabric of work emergencies and off-duty friendship. The memoir ends abruptly and sadly. "One of my comrades in STO [Sojourner Truth Organization], after years in factories, returned to the university.... He urges me to join him.... I take him up on the suggestion.... I manage for a few years to stay in touch with Jackson." Somewhere over the rainbow, way up high, Noel and his friend Jackson are smiling at us, in inter-racial solidarity.

—**Staughton Lynd**, Author of *Solidarity Unionism: Rebuilding the Labor Movement from Below*

My unforgettable friend Noel Ignatiev left us great revolutionary ideas, wonderfully co-edited journals, and brilliantly rendered historical writing. He left a lived example of uncompromising confrontation with power and with stupidity, along with an endless willingness to debate what constituted the latter. Here he leaves us a vivid memoir of the life of a factory and of a revolutionary within it. Full of humanity and humor, it reflects the belief that struggles at the point of production can transform society, the need for radicals to listen and learn, the incredible knowledge workers possess, and the alternating currents of power and pain present in the lives of labor. Ignatiev's signature insistence on the need to disrupt the commitment to whiteness that unites some workers with their bosses is fully made concrete in this lively and marvelous book.

—**David Roediger**, author of *The Sinking Middle Class: A Political History*

Noel's memoir entertains while it instructs. Bringing to life a group of 1970s steel workers in the then "World's Largest Steel Mill," portraits you will not find anywhere else, people whose activities were essential to the nation's economy, but not represented in writings. Noel, always aware of worker's "place" and of course sensitive to role of race, relates tales of daily work that illustrate the important shifts that can occur in consciousness while going about work. One of his favorite quotes was from the Internationale, "We want no condescending saviors." Noel was never condescending, although known to be adamant. This is fun to read.

— **Carole Travis**, with Noel a founder of Sojourner Truth Organization. She worked 20 years at a General Motors Division of locomotive plants, president of that UAW Local representing 10,000 workers for six years until she left in 1992. Those facilities fully closed in 2020.

Noel Ignatiev (1940–2019) was a revolutionary his entire adult life. He worked for 23 years in industry and for 33 years in academia. He was the author of *How the Irish Became White*; co-editor of *Race Traitor*, an American Book Award winner; and editor of *A New Notion: Two Works by C.L.R. James* and *The Lesson of the Hour: Wendell Phillips on Abolition & Strategy*. He was also the founding editor of *Urgent Tasks: Journal of the Revolutionary Left*; *Race Traitor, Journal of the New Abolitionism*; and *Hard Crackers: Chronicles of Everyday Life*.